GOLF FACTS

GOLF
FACTS

Ian Morrison

Grange
BOOKS

A QUANTUM BOOK

Published by Grange Books
An imprint of Grange Books plc
The Grange
Grange Yard
London SE1 3AG

ISBN 1-85627-988-X

QUMGOF

This book was produced by
Quantum Books Ltd
6 Blundell Street
London N7 9BH

Senior Editor Honor Head

Art Editor Philip Gilderdale

Designer Anne Fisher

Illustrator Maps Janos Marffy

Diagrams Kuo Kang Chen

Cartoons Ross Thomson

Picture Manager Rebecca Horsewood

Picture Researcher Mandy Little

Art Director Moira Clinch

Publishing Director Janet Slingsby

Quarto would also like to thank the following for their
assistance: Mr Livingstone, South Herts
Golf Club, London, England and Wilson
Sporting Goods Ltd.

Typeset by En to En Typesetting
Manufactured in Hong Kong by
Regent Publishing Services Ltd.
Printed in Singapore by Star Standard Industries Pte. Ltd

Captions for the pictures on the opening pages at the
beginning of each chapter are as follows: **page 6** Walter
Hagen; **page 7** Early golf ball; **page 16** Jack Nicklaus;
page 42 Nick Price; **page 43** Joyce Wethered; **page 82**
An aerial view of the Pinehurst Golf course in the USA.

CONTENTS

HOW IT ALL STARTED 6

A History of the Game 8 • Joining The Club 10 • Early Tools of the Trade 12
The Development of the Golf Ball 14

PLAYING THE GAME 16

Understanding the Golf Club 18 • Anatomy of a Golf Club 20 • The Hold 22
The Stance and the Address 24 • Swinging the Club 26 • Onto the Fairway 30
Pitching and Chipping 32 • Getting Out of Bunkers 34 • Putting 36
Awkward Shots 38

GOLF GREATS 42

Great Players: Men 44 • Great Players: Women 52 • Great Tours 56
Great Tournaments 64

OUTSTANDING GOLF COURSES 82

AUSTRALIA Royal Melbourne 84 • CANADA Glen Abbey 86 • The National 88 • EIRE
Ballybunion 90 • Portmarnock 91 • ENGLAND The Belfry 92 • Royal Birkdale 94
Royal Liverpool 96 • Royal Lytham 97 • Royal St George's 98 • Sunningdale 99
Wentworth 100 • FRANCE Chantilly 102 • St Nom-la-Breteche 103 • NORTHERN
IRELAND Royal Co. Down 104 • Royal Portrush 106 • PORTUGAL Penina 108
SCOTLAND Carnoustie 110 • Muirfield 112 • Prestwick 114 • Royal Dornoch 115
Royal Troon 116 • St Andrews 118 • Turnberry 120 • SPAIN Valderrama 122
SWITZERLAND Crans-sur-Sierre 124 • UNITED STATES Augusta 126 • Baltusrol 128
• Cypress Point 130 • Inverness 132 • Medinah 134 • Merion 136 • Muirfield Village
138 • Oakhill 140 • Oakland Hills 141 • Oakmont 142 • Olympic 143 • Pebble Beach
144 • Pinehurst 146 • Pine Valley 147 • Shinnecock Hills 148 • Winged Foot 150

Golfing terminology 152 • Index 158 • Acknowledgements 160

How It All Started

THE ORIGIN OF golf is something that historians have been trying to unravel for years, and the definitive answer has not as yet been arrived at. If you think about it logically, we could have been playing golf in prehistoric times. It only needed a stick for use as a club and a stone as a ball and hey presto! one had golf. But many sports can be said to have derived from such ancient origins, so let's look at the realistic claims to golf's origins . . .

A History of the Game

A STAINED-GLASS window installed in Gloucester Cathedral in the mid-14th century depicts a man swinging a stick at a ball. The window was commissioned by Sir Thomas Broadstone, but nothing more is known about the game being played by the man in the window. This could well have been *cambuca*, however, which was a popular stick-and-ball game of the day.

About the same time, in 1353 to be exact, there existed a popular stick-and-ball game in Flanders. The object was to hit the ball across undulating terrain towards a pre-determined goal such as a tree, gate or whatever. This game was called *chole* and certainly bore a resemblance to the modern-day game of golf. So, did the Belgians invent the game? The Dutch also had a similar game called *kolfspel*. Are *they* therefore responsible for giving us golf?

The Scots were certainly playing the game in the 15th century because, in 1457, the first of three Acts of Parliament banning *gouf* was passed. They could have been playing the game for some time before the ban, otherwise the playing of it would hardly have aroused disapproval. Like football, which had been banned thirty years earlier, *gouf* was taking the men

Above A pair of 14th century 'Golfers'.

Right A detail of the window in Gloucester Cathedral clearly depicting a golfer.

Below The entire East Window at Gloucester Cathedral which was installed in the mid-14th century.

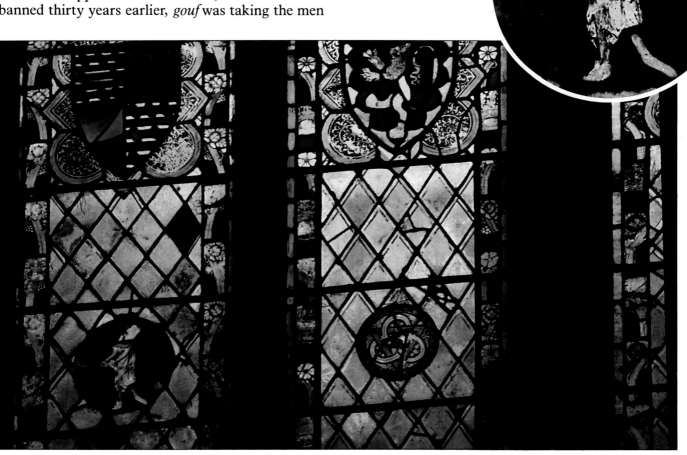

GOLF'S SPORTING QUEEN

Mary, Queen of Scots became Queen of Scotland when she was only six days old, in 1542. She was only 25 when she abdicated but in that time she caused quite a stir both sides of the border and posed a threat to England's Queen, Elizabeth I. It was not only in the royal palaces that Mary attracted a lot of attention but also on the golf links. Furthermore, she was a dab hand at billiards, and when she was held prisoner by Elizabeth I she demanded that a billiard table be installed in her cell.

Mary's second husband was her cousin Henry Stuart, Lord Darnley, but he was murdered in 1567, blown up by gunpowder. Within two weeks of his assassination Mary was out on the golf links at Seton House where she played regularly. This fuelled the belief that she arranged his execution to end their stormy two-year marriage. Mary was herself executed in 1587.

of Scotland away from their much-needed archery practice. Further Acts again banned *gouf* in 1470 and 1491. The last was passed by James IV, but ten years later it is recorded that he bought himself a set of golf clubs! Royal approval at last!

The birthright of golf has, therefore, not been precisely established. But one thing is certain: Scotland is the "home" of golf, and it was from there that the game spread to become one of the most international of all sports.

The Archbishop of St Andrews gave his approval for the people of the Burgh to play golf over the local links in 1553, and fourteen years later Mary, Queen of Scots became one of golf's best-known exponents.

Royalty and nobility were soon followed as golfing enthusiasts by other members of the community and in a short time links were being developed all over Scotland. And with its increased popularity there came the need for organized clubs and, of course, the inevitable set of rules.

JOINING THE CLUB

THE FIRST GOLF CLUB, the Edinburgh Golfing Society, later the Royal Burgess Golfing Society of Edinburgh, was founded in 1743, the year before the formation of the Gentlemen Golfers of Edinburgh (later the Honourable Company of Edinburgh Golfers), who were responsible for drawing up golf's first set of rules - all 13 of them.

Ten years after the Honourable Company's birth, the St Andrews Club (later the Royal and Ancient) was formed and their original set of rules was almost identical to the Honourable Company's.

While the rules had become standardized, the number of holes had not. The Honourable Company's original links at Leith consisted of five holes, while St Andrews' original course had 12 greens and a total of 22 holes. It was reduced to 18 holes in 1764 and, because of their stature, other clubs eventually followed suit, either extending or reducing their courses to 18 holes like St Andrews.

While it is recorded that the Prince of Wales played golf at Greenwich around 1608, the sport's rapid spread south of the border came in the latter half of the 18th century following the formation of

THE WORLD'S OLDEST GOLF CLUBS

1735	Royal Burgess Golfing Society of Edinburgh (a)
1744	Honourable Company of Edinburgh Golfers
1754	Royal and Ancient (St Andrews)
1761	Bruntsfield Links Golfing Society
1766	Royal Blackheath (b)
1774	Royal Musselburgh
1780	Royal Aberdeen
1787	Glasgow Gailes
1787	Glasgow Killermont
1791	Cruden Bay (Aberdeenshire)

(a) The Royal Burgess Golfing Society of Edinburgh is credited with being formed in 1735 as the Edinburgh Golf Society, and did not assume the title of Edinburgh Burgess until 1787. Most sources accept that the oldest golf club in the world is therefore Honourable Company of Edinburgh Golfers.

(b) The exact date of the formation of the Blackheath Club is uncertain and some sources record that golf was played there in the 17th century by James VI of Scotland. However, it is generally accepted that the club was formed in 1766.

Left Four gentlemen golfers, with their caddies, playing at the St Andrews links in 1798. Note how the four players are dressed alike as are the caddies.

England's first club, Royal Blackheath, in 1766.

As Britons set sail for other continents, many of them took their bag of golf clubs with them and spread the golfing word. The Calcutta Club in India (later the Royal Calcutta Club) became the first organized club outside Britain in 1829, and in 1856 the Pau club in France became the first on the mainland of Europe.

From there, the sport spread rapidly and by the turn of the century it was being played in many corners of the globe.

Australia's first club, the Adelaide, was formed in 1870. New Zealand had its first organized club at Dunedin a year later and inevitably the sport found its way to North America, where the Montreal Club was formed in 1873.

Perhaps surprisingly, early attempts to develop the game in the United States had failed. The Crail Golfing Society in South Carolina was formed in 1786, but it did not last. Neither did the Oakhurst Club in Virginia, which was formed in 1884. However, four years later golf "arrived" in the USA when the St Andrews Club at Yonkers, New York was formed. In 1894 the United States Golf Association was founded and they remain the ruling body for the game in North America.

Like many other nations, the USA inaugurated their own Championships following the lead of the Prestwick Club, who started the British Open Championship in 1860.

DID YOU KNOW?

The first book about golf was The Golfer's Manual published in 1857. Its author, H B Farnie, used the pen-name "A Keen Hand".

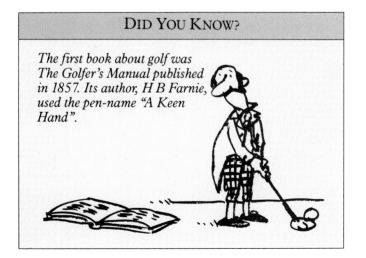

THE HONOURABLE COMPANY

The Society of the Gentlemen Golfers of Edinburgh was formed on 1 May 1744 under their first president Duncan Forbes of Culloden. There is evidence to suggest that golf had been played over five holes at the Leith links before that date, but 1744 is when they are officially credited with forming their Society. In this year the Provost of Edinburgh donated a splendid silver golf club as a trophy, to be contested for annually. It remains one of the most cherished of all golfing trophies. Not only did the annual winner receive the silver trophy but he was also designated the "captain of the club" and was responsible for resolving all golfing disputes amongst members. Consequently, the Gentlemen Golfers drew up the game's first set of rules.

In 1759 they were granted permission to adopt the title the Honourable Company of Edinburgh Golfers. Sadly, they ceased to exist in 1831 and wound up their affairs. But after five years they were re-formed with Musselburgh as their new home. In 1891 they moved further down the East Lothian coast to their present home at Muirfield and the following year played hosts to the British Open for the first time.

EARLY TOOLS OF THE TRADE

THE PIONEERING GOLFERS of 200 years ago did not have the benefits of graphite-shafted clubs and the like that have developed to aid modern-day golfers. And they did not have skilfully manicured greens and well-cut fairways to play on. In the mid 1800s there was no finer golfer than Young Tom Morris, but he never shot 18-hole rounds of 63 and 64, which the likes of Nick Faldo and Seve Ballesteros can do today with such regularity.

Almost certainly, early golf clubs were made of wood. There is no documented evidence to suggest what they were made of prior to the 18th century. But when the likes of the Honourable Company and St Andrews clubs were formed, all clubs were wooden, with hazel and ash being the most popular for the shafts. Beech, apple, pear or blackthorn were popular choices for the head, depending on whether

BAFFY, BRASSIE AND MASHIE

Golf clubs in days gone by had some lovely names. Sadly they are no longer with us, and they have been replaced by simple descriptions like 2-wood, 4-iron, wedge and so on. The following list is of old clubs and their modern-day equivalents:

Old name	Current equivalent
Baffing Spoon (wood)	9-iron/wedge
Baffy	4-wood
Blaster	Sand wedge
Brassie	2-wood
Cleek	2-iron
Jigger (also known as a Sammy)	4-iron
Mashie	5-iron
Mashie-niblick	7-iron
Niblick	8/9-iron
Play Club	Driver
Spoon	3-wood

Left A selection of some early hickory-shafted clubs.

Right Major Boothby about to play a shot from close to the Swilcan Burn at St Andrews. Watching is Old Tom Morris (left) and Allan Robertson (on bridge with single club).

the club was for driving, playing fairway or approach shots, or putting. The head and shaft were glued together and bound in twine.

The day of the 14-club golfer was a long way off. Most top golfers would have five or six clubs at the most. But the top players soon realized there was a need to have a different club for each type of shot, and they soon started having clubs made with different lofts.

When the gutty arrived, it put a lot of strain on the club and it was at that time that iron-headed models gained in popularity. Hickory was used for the shafts instead of hazel or ash. By the end of the 19th century club heads were becoming more standard in shape and size; top players used eight or nine clubs and their caddies had special bags in which to carry them.

After the Haskell ball became popular it was necessary to find another wood suitable for the wooden-headed clubs because the ball was causing damage to the traditional heads. And the North American wood persimmon was found to be ideal. However, damage was still being caused to the face of the club and, consequently, ivory or bone inserts were built in.

Because of the game's popularity, golf club manufacture was moving away from individual hand-made pieces of craftsmanship towards mass production. And when hickory was in short supply after World War I, manufacturers turned to steel-shafted clubs. They were given their seal of approval by the US Professional Golf Association (USPGA) in 1924 and by the Royal & Ancient (R & A) in Scotland six years later.

Mass-produced clubs changed the whole shape of the game, as it was possible to produce matched sets. For the first time players were able to carry a set of matching clubs which differed only in length and loft. Weight, appearance and feel of the club were the same and this led to a marked improvement in the standard of play amongst professionals and amateurs alike.

Modern day golf clubs have seen persimmon woods replaced by laminated plastic and subsequently light aluminium heads, and the steel shafts have made way for the more supple graphite and titanium shafts. One-piece clubs with the head and shaft working as a single unit give the golfer a closer relationship between club and ball. And cavity-back irons, with the backs hollowed out and with scientifically calculated centres of gravity to give a more controlled feel of the club, are essential to the 1990s golf professional - the day of the "game improving" club is upon us. One has to wonder what the likes of Young Tom Morris could have achieved with a bag of 1990s golf clubs.

THE DEVELOPMENT OF THE GOLF BALL

THE EARLIEST GOLF BALLS were carved out of wood. You can imagine how "round" they were! There were no such things as precision tools in those days. The first breakthrough in golf ball manufacture came with the introduction of the "feathery", which was first seen in the 15th century. Each ball was made by stuffing a top-hatful of feathers into a leather casing which was then rounded and hand stitched. No two balls weighed the same and their shape varied as well - and by quite a lot after a round of golf!

A major step forward was made in 1848 when the Reverend Robert Preston invented the "gutty", which was moulded out of **gutta-percha,** a gum substance from Malaya. The first gutty was used at the Blackheath Club and, because it was round and

thus gave the ball a true flight, it became very popular.

One problem with this new ball was that it fell from the sky like a dead bird without completing its true trajectory. However, this problem mysteriously cured itself towards the end of a round when it was realized that this was because of the damage done to the ball during the round. It was decided to manufacture golf balls with the "damage" already done, and so the "dimpled" golf ball was born.

The gutty was eventually phased out after the American Coburn Haskell developed the rubber-cored ball in 1898. His ball failed to receive the immediate acclaim of the day's top professionals, but when Alex Herd won the 1902 British Open, after outdriving his rivals, that all changed. There was a

Above Two 'featheries' used in the 1840s.

Right This top hat full of feathers was required to make one 'feathery' ball.

rush to get hold of a Haskell ball, which was made by wrapping an elastic thread around a rubber core and coating it in dimpled plastic. This was the three-piece ball and manufacturers were, and still are, constantly experimenting with dimple design and arrangement in an effort to design a ball that will achieve ever-greater distance.

The three-piece ball has, however, made way for the two-piece in recent years, consisting of a single-piece acrylate core coated in a dimpled cover. Yet another improvement to help the present-day golfer.

Top The evolution of the golf ball from the original wooden ball through to the rubber-core ball.

Above A golf ball press.

Above Willie Park Senior, the first Open champion.

Left What the late 19th century golfer looked like. Willie Park Junior with caddie John Carey.

PLAYING THE GAME

IT IS IMPORTANT that any budding golfer should realize from the outset that the likes of Nick Faldo, Jack Nicklaus, Arnold Palmer, Tom Watson, Seve Ballesteros and Curtis Strange didn't suddenly become good golfers. They have spent many years developing their already innate skills. True, the high handicap golfer will go out and hit the occasional wonderful drive straight down the middle of the fairway. And true, he will think "this is easy". But what happens next? He approaches his second shot with a 4-iron, slices it out of bounds, and it's back to the drawing board.

To get from tee to green is *not* easy, and in this chapter we will attempt to familiarize you with the basic golf swing, highlight the common errors that creep into one's game, and hopefully point you in the right direction towards making that short journey from tee to green.

UNDERSTANDING THE GOLF CLUB

MANY PEOPLE, WHEN they decide to take up golf, go out and spend a lot of money on equipment without really understanding what they are buying.

Because golf equipment *is* expensive it is important to know what to look for. A look through any golf magazine and you will be lost in a maze of graphite shafts, persimmon heads, single-unit clubs, cavity-back irons and so on. Indeed these are all modern-day technological improvements which are designed to make the game easier, and they do work. But the best tools in the hand of a poor craftsman don't guarantee good work. Likewise with golf clubs.

THE FIRST STEP: WHAT TO BUY

If you look at a full set of clubs laid out in a shop you will instantly see that each is a different length. But don't forget, sets do come in different lengths. So, just because a set of clubs look good and feel good on the grip, they may not be the right length for you. A further look at each club reveals that the lie (angle between shaft and head) varies and this lie alters the swing path. So, you must know which lie is ideal for your swing path. You must be sure to select clubs with the right lie for your height and physique.

So where do you go for the correct advice? Any PGA professional will be only too pleased to advise on the correct clubs for you, a service that many retail outlets often do not provide. But this advice is important. You are making a big investment when you buy a set of golf clubs and you and your clubs have got to be compatible.

DO YOU NEED A FULL SET OF CLUBS?

The simple rule is "buy within your budget". But remember, the most clubs you are allowed to carry in your bag is 14. The top professionals carry the maximum but they know exactly what they can achieve with each club. The club player with a full set will use only half of them on a regular basis, will occasionally give the others an airing, play a bad shot, and leave them in the bag for six months.

Ideally a half set, consisting of a 3-wood, 3-, 5-, 7- and 9-irons, a sand wedge, and a putter, is enough for the novice to get going. Of course, the more you play and the more you enjoy the game (and maybe get better at it as well) then you will want to increase your number of clubs. But for the time being, settle for a half set.

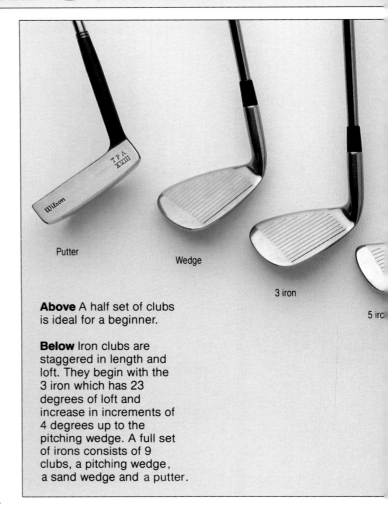

Putter   Wedge   3 iron   5 iron

Above A half set of clubs is ideal for a beginner.

Below Iron clubs are staggered in length and loft. They begin with the 3 iron which has 23 degrees of loft and increase in increments of 4 degrees up to the pitching wedge. A full set of irons consists of 9 clubs, a pitching wedge, a sand wedge and a putter.

7 iron

9 iron

3 wood

THE MODERN DAY GOLF BALL

As manufacturers constantly attempt to keep up to date with modern technology they are always seeking to make the game of golf easier for all players at all levels, particularly professionals.

Golf ball manufacture is one area where time and money is regularly spent researching the effect of differently designed balls. A great deal of attention is placed on dimple design and placement, both of which affect the path, distance and trajectory of the ball. Indeed, some balls are designed to fit the appropriate shot. Those with softer outer cases like the Balata ball, allow for greater control and backspin when playing approach shots to the green. But the practice of professional players using one ball for short holes and changing it when playing long holes is rightly being outlawed by the controlling bodies.

With modern balls being assembled in two pieces, attention is paid to the compression of the inner part of the ball without compressing it too much or too little. Balls with a greater compression ratio should, when hit correctly, travel further than one with a low ratio. But hit it wrong, and boy, can it hurt!

But the key to all this rests on the ability and skill of the man with the club in his hands. A good quality high compression ball in the hands of a man who hasn't a clue what to do with the club is a waste of time and money.

DID YOU KNOW?

A Japanese company is planning to introduce a new golfing product - the biodegradable tee. Usually made of wood or plastic, many tees are lost during the course of a game disfiguring golf courses. Apparently the Japanese version turns into compost within hours.

ANATOMY OF A GOLF CLUB

THE GOLF CLUB consists of a head, shaft and handle. As mentioned earlier, modern-day designs provide a wide choice for all golfers, professional and amateur alike. But, no matter whether you select steel shafted, graphite shafted, wooden heads, aluminium heads, the make-up of the golf club is the same.

The **handle** is the part of the club you hold and is known as the grip. A look at the grip and you will see a pattern on it. This pattern is not just to make it look pretty but is to help you make sure your club is aligned properly when addressing the ball. If the pattern is off-centre then you have not addressed the ball in the correct manner.

The **club face** is made up of the face, the toe, the heel and the most important part the **leading edge**. The leading edge is the bottom edge of the club face and it is this part of the club head that must be lined up with the ball and square to it and the ball-to-target line at address. Many novices believe the top of the club should be used to square up against the ball at address. This is wrong. It is important *now* that you understand the leading edge because it forms the basis of every golf shot. The leading edge is *always* at right angles to the ball and ball-to-target line (which will be explained in greater detail later) no matter whether you are playing with an open or closed club face.

Grip

Shaft

Iron

Wood

Right A full set of clubs contains a maximum of 14 clubs. The average set consists of 3-9 irons, 1 and 5 woods, (the 1 wood is also known as the driver) a pitching wedge, sand wedge and putter. The driver shown here is an oversized-head driver.

Below A close-up of a wooden clubhead. The leading edge is probably the most important part of it.

Roof

Toe

Heel

Leading edge

Oversized-head driver

3 wood

5 wood

1 iron

7 iron

5 iron

3 iron

Sand wedge

6 iron

8 iron

4 iron

Wedge

9 iron

Putter

THE HOLD

THE FIRST STEP towards mastering the basic golf swing, is to learn the hold. The left hand (assuming you are a right-handed player) is the more important of the two hands in the hold. It is the dominant hand yet only the 3rd, 4th and 5th fingers actually grip the club.

To establish the correct hold, open your left hand and diagonally place the club handle across the palm. Close your hand, making sure the last three fingers only grip the handle. Your other finger, and thumb, merely play a "supporting" role - literally.

To check if you are holding the club correctly with your left hand, ground the club head in the address position, and keeping your left arm straight, you will see that a "v" has been formed by your thumb and index finger. If you are holding the club correctly this "v" should be pointing to a spot between your head and right shoulder.

Now for the right hand. This time only the second and third fingers apply pressure on the handle. The other fingers, and thumb, are again to give support. But where exactly do you put all of your fingers? Well, there are three basic holds, and each is designed to suit personal needs depending on the size of your hands. Try all three before you find the one you feel most comfortable with. However, none feel all that comfortable at first.

THE OVERLAPPING HOLD

Often referred to as "The Vardon Grip" after champion golfer Harry Vardon who popularized the hold at the turn of the century, this is the most popular of the three holds. Having applied pressure with the second and third fingers of your right hand, the little finger rests on top of the forefinger of your left hand. Ground the club as before and this time you will see that both hands have created a "v" as previously mentioned. And for the hold to be correct *both* "v"s must be aiming towards that point between your head and right shoulder.

THE INTERLOCKING HOLD

Popular among golfers with smaller hands, this hold is similar to the overlapping hold but this time the little finger of the right hand and forefinger of the left are interlocked. Again, check that your "v"s are pointing in the right place.

ESTABLISHING THE HOLD

To establish the correct grip, take the club in your left hand (below left), making sure it is comfortable. Close your hand (below right). Place the club handle in your right hand as shown (near right). The second and third fingers only of the right hand should apply pressure. Finally, adopt the address position (far right). Note that your right shoulder will dip slightly once this position has been established.

THE TWO-HANDED HOLD

This is sometimes called the "double-handed grip" because all fingers of both hands make contact with the club handle and with one hand above the other. This hold is the least popular and least used of the three but is often used by people who are unable to place a strong hold on the handle.

The key thing to remember with the hold is those "v"s. Make sure they are always aiming to that point between your head and right shoulder. This applies no matter what club you are using. Wayward shots can be caused by many factors but more often than not they stem from the very beginning - the hold. So make sure it is right from the start.

Of course, the foregoing will be the opposite way round if you are left-handed. However, for the purpose of the remainder of the book we will assume you are right-handed - it makes life a lot easier.

The two-handed hold.

The overlapping hold, known as the Vardon Grip.

The interlocking hold with the index finger of the left hand and little finger of the right hand interlocking.

THE STANCE AND THE ADDRESS

THE CORRECT STANCE and address are vital to achieve your ball-to-target line via the correct swing path. The **ball-to-target line** is the direction in which you intend to send the ball towards a predetermined target.

There are three types of **swing path**: *inside-to-square*, *out-to-in* and *in-to-out*. But, to understand what that is all about you must first understand what is meant by *outside* and *inside*.

When you take up your normal stance your feet are *inside* the ball-to-target line. The area the other side of the ball-to-target line is the *outside*.

The normal golf stroke follows a path whereby the clubhead is taken back on the *inside*, is brought down, makes contact with the ball and follows through on the *inside*. This is known as the *inside-to-square* swing path. A clubhead taken back on the outside but travelling inside on the follow-through is known as an *out-to-in* swing path and the *in-to-out* path is the opposite.

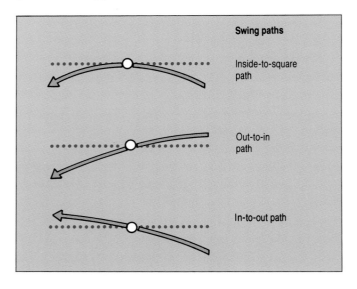

Swing paths

Inside-to-square path

Out-to-in path

In-to-out path

THE STANCE

You are probably familiar with the "keep the left arm straight" theory. Well, the left arm does have to be kept straight most of the time, but don't fall into the trap of believing the left arm and club must be kept straight and rigid as one unit. They don't.

To adopt the correct position of your left arm, hold it down by your side. Now clench your fist as if you were holding a club, and then insert a club into the clenched hand. You will see that an angle has been created between your left arm and the club.

This is the correct setting of the left arm and that is how your left arm and club should look when the ball is being addressed. This is where novices fall down; they believe the left arm should be straight *and* the club should be an extension of that arm as one straight unit.

Bob Tway, the surprise winner of the 1986 US PGA Championship, defied all the rules of the basic swing. His stance was cumbersome, he had a hunched back and placed his hands low down the club handle. Yet he won a Major.

You are now holding the club correctly, and have adopted the correct left arm position. Now it is time to address the ball.

THE ADDRESS

It is important to get your posture correct at address. Don't bend your knees too much: this is a common fault with high-handicap golfers. They tend to think that the knees are the most important part of the body in the address position. They are not. That privilege belongs to the spine. It is important that you obtain the correct spinal angle.

To obtain the correct spinal angle, stand upright and bend your back forward slightly so that your backside is sticking out slightly. Now bend your

Head behind ball

Right shoulder lower than left

Left arm not quite straight

Correct grip

Slightly bent knees

Feet parallel to ball-to- target line

Above Note how the head is behind the ball, the distance between the feet, and the position of the ball in relation to the left heel.

Right This picture shows that the left arm and club are not one straight unit.

knees, and you have adopted the correct posture. Try and imagine yourself sitting on the edge of a high stool - that is what the correct posture should be.

Your hold is now right, left arm is OK, and posture is fine. But that is not the end of it. We now have to make sure the shoulders are in the right position. The shoulders are an integral part of the golf swing. If they aren't working properly then the whole swing will fall apart. There is a lot to learn about this golf swing, but, if you get it right at the outset, you will always have a good swing.

The ideal shoulder position should be with your right shoulder slightly lower than your left. This is achieved by moving your head so that it is slightly behind the ball in the address position. If it is not behind the ball this will result in an unbalanced swing, and this means problems.

The head plays a very crucial role in the golf swing. How often have you heard the expression "he lifted his head too quickly"? People don't say that for the sake of it. Poor use of the head *does* result in a poor golf shot.

The head should be kept in the same position, slightly behind the golf ball, throughout the swing and even at the moment the club and ball make contact. It should only be lifted on the follow-through after impact. But we will come to that later. So: *don't move your head during the swing.*

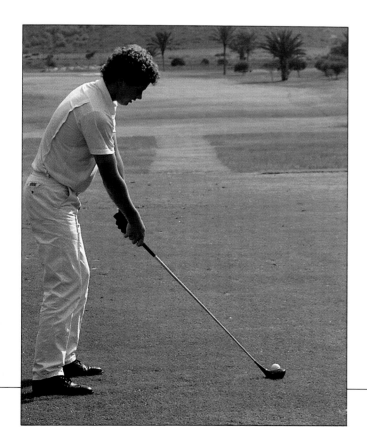

YOUR QUESTIONS ANSWERED

Q **How do I establish the ball-to-target line?**

A Imagine a straight line drawn from the ball to the target. That is the ball-to-target line. But to make sure you are standing in the correct position at address you must be standing parallel to the ball-to-target line to establish what is called a **square stance**. Therefore, imagine another line drawn in front of your feet. This line should be parallel to the ball-to-target line. If your left foot is drawn back from this line then you are said to have adopted an **open stance** and your entire body will be aiming to the left of the intended target. A **closed stance** is when the left foot is forward of the right and the body is pointing towards the right of the intended target.

Having adopted a correct square stance, line the club up with the ball, making sure the leading edge is square to the ball and ball-to-target line.

Q **How far apart should my feet be when addressing the ball?**

A There is no golden rule on this subject. The choice of club and your own physical make-up will dictate this to a large extent. But, as a general rule, the inside of your shoes should be level with your shoulders when playing with a wooden club and when you use a short iron, like a wedge, then the outside of your shoes should be level with your shoulders. But the secret is to be comfortable.

Q **How high should I tee the ball when driving?**

A If using a wood the general rule is to make sure about half of the ball is showing above the top of the clubhead. But this is only a guideline. If you are playing into a strong headwind you would tee the ball up lower than usual. The most important rule is *not to tee the ball too high.* When using irons you don't need to tee the ball as high as when using a wooden club.

SWINGING THE CLUB

IF, AFTER DIGESTING the foregoing about hold, posture, head position and so on, you still want to play golf then read on. But be warned, there is still much more to learn about the golf swing!

There is only one golf swing - whether you are playing a full blooded drive off the tee or a 9-iron approach shot to the green, the swing is the same, although modified to fit the shot.

The first action of the golf swing after address is the takeaway and, like all other aspects of the swing, it is crucial that you have a good takeaway. Get that wrong and the chance of the remainder of the swing being wrong is very high.

The takeaway is achieved by taking the clubhead backwards from the ball and at the same time rotating the entire left side of your body towards the right which is possible because your right hip and shoulder move backwards slightly at the same time

as the takeaway. It is important to make sure that your elbows are kept the same distance apart during the takeaway as they were at address.

THE BACKSWING

The takeaway is the first part of the backswing, which follows on in one continuous and fluent movement as you take the club above your head.

A successful backswing is achieved by correctly cocking the wrists at the right time. The wrists should cock naturally during the backswing, and the shorter the club the earlier they cock. With a driver they do not cock until nearly at the top of the backswing.

We have already mentioned about keeping the left arm straight, and it should be kept straight at all

THE BLUEPRINT GOLF SWING

Here we see a classic golf swing from the address, through the takeaway and backswing, to the downswing and follow-through.

Shoulders

Hips

Knees

Feet

Comfortable address - not too tense.

Straight left arm on takeaway

Head behind the ball and kept still. Right elbow pointing at the ground behind the right heel.

Weight transferred to the left leg immediately before contact.

times, although it is not necessary for it to be rigid. At the top of the backswing it is virtually impossible to keep it rigidly straight even if you try. Keep it as straight as you can, but feel comfortable.

At the top of the backswing your right elbow should be pointing towards the ground slightly behind your right heel and the club shaft should be pointing towards the target and parallel to the ball-to-target line. Your elbows should have kept the same distance apart throughout the backswing.

There is no need to rush the takeaway and backswing. Take a look at Larry Nelson. His takeaway is so deliberate, as is his backswing, and they result in a lovely rhythmic swing. Top US money winner Corey Pavin also has a fluent swing, and on the European Tour Sam Torrance boasts one of the best swings, thanks to his slow deliberate action. Ian Woosnam also has a fluent swing, which

he makes look so easy. But what awesome power the little man can pack into those clubs.

Once the clubhead has reached the top of the backswing, it has to start its return journey to the ball, the downswing, which, like all other aspects of the swing, is very important, because everything must come down as it went up for the clubhead to make the correct contact with the ball.

THE DOWNSWING

The hips play a key role in the downswing and they move slightly ahead of your hands so that the weight can be transferred from your right side to your left leg, which will enable you to keep your body square with the ball at impact. It is important that you keep your head still during the downswing and that you

Shoulders

Hips

Knees

Feet

Head remains still and everything is back to where it started at address.

The follow through starts.

The club is raised, and the head automatically starts to lift as the eyes begin to follow the ball.

The end of the swing. The clubhead is behind the head and the toes of the right foot point towards the ground maintain the correct spinal angle.

You may think that is the end of the swing. But it is not. The swing doesn't end at the moment the clubhead makes contact with the ball. There is also the very important follow-through to mention.

THE FOLLOW-THROUGH

After making contact with the ball, allow the clubhead to continue on its natural journey until it swings behind your head. As you follow-through, the action will automatically lift your head, so there is no need to lift it early to see where your ball has gone. Many novices make the mistake of lifting their head as soon as contact is made with the ball. A good follow-through will bring your head up automatically and at the right time. If you have followed through correctly your balance will be transferred entirely to your left leg and your right knee will be facing the target and the balance of your right leg transferred to your right toe.

Two final tips on the swing.

• Always keep your eye on the ball but remember, when playing your shot, you should concentrate on looking at the back of the ball.

• Maintain a good balance through the entire swing. To test your balance, try and hold your follow-through position until the ball has landed. If you can manage this, give yourself a pat on the back: you have maintained perfect balance.

Johnny Miller executes an impressive follow-through at the 1991 Open at Birkdale.

YOUR QUESTIONS ANSWERED

Q How do I cure slicing and hooking?

A Slicing off the tee is probably the most common fault that novices encounter. And when you look at the list of possible causes it is hardly surprising that the slice occurs. The most common fault is striking the ball with an open club face. In other words, the leading edge is not at right angles to the ball and ball-to-target line. Instead, it is pointing to the right of the target. This is often caused by a poor takeaway or a weak hold with one or both hands too far around the club handle.

An incorrect address position, normally by having the ball too far forward in relation to your feet, will lead to the slice. This is because the shoulders are open, and not square at address. An open stance is also a likely cause of the slice.

Again, there are many possible causes of the hook. This time, a strong hold, with one or both hands too far to the right around the handle, will be a likely cause. Closed shoulders at address will probably cause a hook, which will stem from having the ball positioned too far back at address.

Having the left elbow too close to the body in the back- and downswing are other common causes, as is over-swinging at the top of the backswing, when the club goes too far at the top of the swing and is pointing to the right of the intended target. But the most common cause of the hook is the closed clubface at impact. Check to see where your hands are at address. If they are too far forward then it is a simple matter to rectify.

Q What is a push shot? Is it like a slice?

A No, it isn't like a slice. A slice is when the ball starts by aiming towards the intended target but then veers right. The push is when the ball travels to the right of the intended target but in a straight line. This is more often than not caused by incorrect alignment with the ball-to-target line at address.

Q Is the pull therefore the opposite to the push?

A Yes, except this time the ball is "pulled" to the left of the target instead of the right with the push. Like the push, it is often a well struck shot, but alignment at address was all wrong.

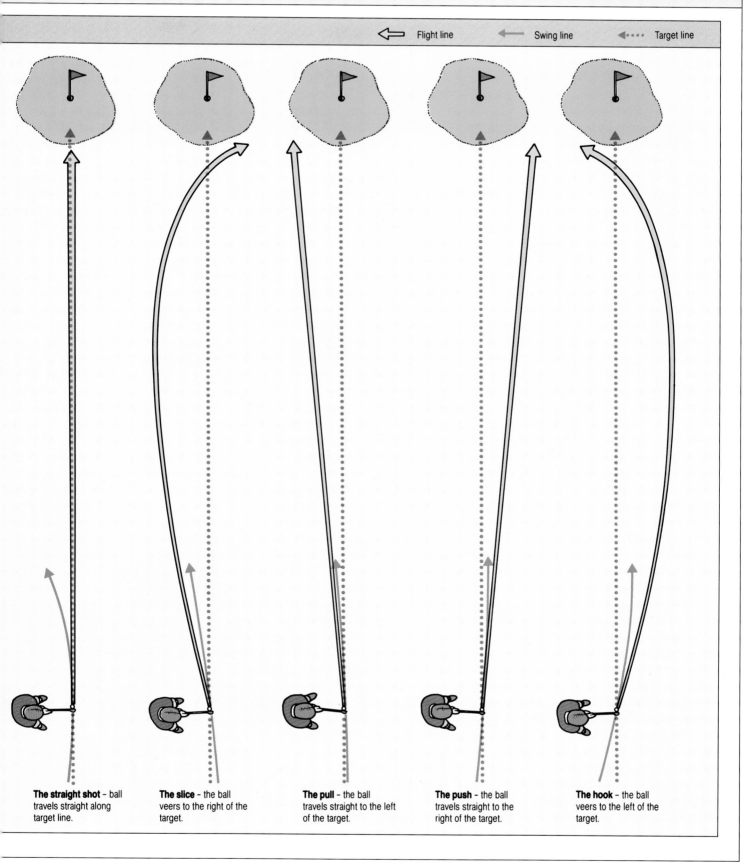

Flight line   Swing line   Target line

The straight shot – ball travels straight along target line.

The slice - the ball veers to the right of the target.

The pull – the ball travels straight to the left of the target.

The push – the ball travels straight to the right of the target.

The hook - the ball veers to the left of the target.

ONTO THE FAIRWAY

PROVIDED YOU HAVE mastered the basic swing, all other golf shots should now become a mere formality. But there are certain pointers that you should bear in mind when adapting the basic swing to specific shots.

PLAYING FAIRWAY WOODS

Many high-handicap golfers find the use of the fairway wood for extra distance an awesome prospect. But, if you have the blueprint swing correct then it need not be and, if played correctly, you will gain some extra valuable yards each round. Don't, however, think that you have to use a wood every time you are on the fairway. You have to analyse your next shot and decide whether a wood will be more beneficial to you than an iron. But only you can make that decision when faced with your next shot.

The position of your ball on the fairway will dictate whether you take a wood or iron. If you have a poor lie then leave the wood in your bag. However, if your ball is lying in a good position, take the wood out if you feel it will benefit you. But don't think you are the next Nick Faldo or Jack Nicklaus by taking out your No. 1 wood. Try a more lofted club like a 2-, 3-, 4- or 5-wood. The best tip when deciding whether to play the wood is make sure the leading edge sits nicely on the ground. If it does, then you should be OK with the club. If not, seriously consider changing it. It is also advisable to slightly, but only slightly, close your stance when playing fairway woods. This will help you to get your right shoulder out of the way during the backswing.

PLAYING LONG IRONS

The long irons are those between a 1- and 4-iron. Again, a slightly closed stance should be adopted so that you can get your right shoulder out of the way in the backswing. Other than that, play the shot as normal and remember, because you are playing a long iron, you need to play the shot with a full swing. Remember, the longer the iron, the nearer to your left heel the ball should be at address. As you use the 4-iron, then the position of the ball should be moving nearer to a position midway between your two feet. But, if you have adopted the correct hold and posture, then this should now become second nature.

One of the best long-iron players is Britain's Sandy Lyle. He generates a great deal of power, but a close look at his swing reveals a gentle and smooth takeaway, the start of any successful swing.

PLAYING THE MEDIUM IRONS

The medium irons are regarded as the 5-, 6- and 7-irons. By now, the ball position at address should have moved towards the centre of your feet with it moving slightly nearer to your right foot with the 7-iron. But, don't forget, you must also make sure your head is still behind the ball. The temptation is now to move it over the ball. Resist it!

You will have noticed that the clubs are now getting shorter. Consequently, when you adopt your stance you will find yourself standing closer to the ball. Furthermore the gap between your feet will

PLAYING WITH FAIRWAY WOODS

Playing with a fairway wood is little different from playing a wood off the tee. The position of the ball in relation to the left heel should be the same and the width of shoulders should be equivalent to the width between the insides of your feet.

Stance and posture remain the same when playing fairway woods. A slightly, but only *slightly*, closed stance will help the swing.

have closed and your shoulders should now be, approximately, level with the outside of your shoes.

There is no need to adopt a slightly closed stance when playing medium irons; you should adopt a square stance and because the clubs are now shorter, your stance will be more upright and this will result in you making a shorter swing.

PLAYING WITH SHORT IRONS

The other irons, 8- and 9-iron, and the two wedges are regarded as the short irons.

The feet are moved closer together when playing with these irons, the ball is in a position closer to the right heel and a slightly open stance is adopted. When taking a very short swing you need to get your body out of the way quickly after making contact with the ball and a slightly open stance helps.

PLAYING WITH SHORT IRONS

When playing irons, the shorter the iron, the closer the feet are positioned together. The outside of the shoes should be level with your shoulders.

The shorter the iron, the nearer you should stand to the ball at address. But length of club dictates this distance. Open your stance slightly when playing with shorter irons. It will help to get the left side of your body out of the way quicker in the backswing.

YOUR QUESTIONS ANSWERED

Q I find that I often top the ball when playing a fairway wood or with a 1- or 2-iron. Why is this?

A First of all, it is important to realize that you don't have to lift the ball into the air – the club is designed to do that for you. That already gets rid of one of the causes of topping, trying to lift the ball off the ground.

Having the ball too far forward or standing too far away from the ball at address are two major causes of topping. Poor weight distribution during the back- and downswing will result in your head coming up too soon. The result – topping.

Playing with a tense hold is often a cause of topping, but many players don't realize they are gripping too tightly. This results in the whole body becoming tense, which results in an upward movement of the body at the moment of contact. If you do realize you are feeling tense at address then walk away from your address position and start all over again. It is remarkable how much difference it will make to your play if you are relaxed at address.

Of course, one very simple cause of topping is taking the wrong club to a ball in relation to its lie. You wouldn't dream of taking a 2-wood to a ball plugged in a rainsoaked fairway. So *don't*.

Q And what about fluffing?

A Fluffing is another of those embarrassing shots that creeps into the novice's game. It is when the clubhead strikes the ground at the back of the ball before making contact with it. The most common cause is having the ball positioned too far back at address. To then compensate, the back- and downswing have to be altered and it results in a last-minute stabbing at the ball, with disastrous consequences.

Q Why am I now taking divots with medium and short irons?

A Because your swing is now more of an upright one, and the angle the clubhead approaches the ball creates a divot. Don't worry, there is nothing wrong with taking a divot but *you must always, repeat, always, replace any divots* you take. Golf courses take plenty of hammering as it is. Try and spare them a bit by replacing your own divots and any left by other inconsiderate golfers.

PITCHING AND CHIPPING

FIRST OF ALL, it is important to appreciate the difference between pitching and chipping. The **pitch** is played by using a lofted club (9-iron or wedge, or similar) on to the green. Depending upon conditions and amount of backspin applied to the ball, it will either stop dead on landing, roll or spin forward slightly or even roll or spin backwards. The **chip**, however, is played with a less lofted club and is played on to the green but then runs on towards the target.

The decision whether to pitch or chip rests solely with you. But, don't forget, course conditions must be taken into account. A rock-hard putting surface is not the best to pitch to because the ball will probably run on after pitching. In this case a delicate chip and run will be the best shot. A damp fairway and green will lend itself better to the pitch as will a ball sitting up nicely in lush grass. And don't forget, if it is a windy day, then a pitched ball will be affected by it.

The pitch is played only with the arms and hands; the full golf swing is not necessary. But all the other rules of the swing apply. Don't try and play a full-blooded swing; it is not necessary because the pitch is only made when the ball has just a small distance to travel.

Make sure the leading edge is square to the ball and ball-to-target line, and open your stance slightly, because you have to transfer your weight from your right leg to your left quicker than normal because of the shortness of the backswing. But remember, there will be very little transfer of weight when playing a pitch or chip. When playing short pitches on to the green shorten your club slightly by moving your hands down the handle.

When playing a lofted shot, the ball will make a pitch mark on the green. Before you make your putt,

---

YOUR QUESTIONS ANSWERED

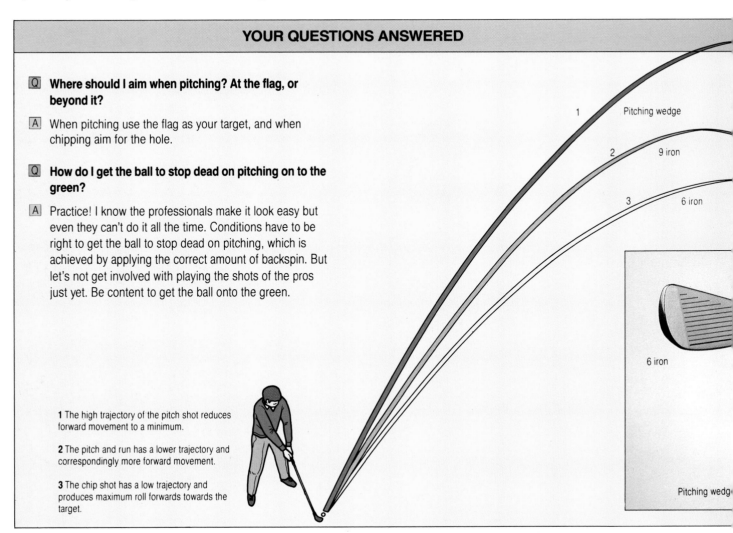

Q Where should I aim when pitching? At the flag, or beyond it?

A When pitching use the flag as your target, and when chipping aim for the hole.

Q How do I get the ball to stop dead on pitching on to the green?

A Practice! I know the professionals make it look easy but even they can't do it all the time. Conditions have to be right to get the ball to stop dead on pitching, which is achieved by applying the correct amount of backspin. But let's not get involved with playing the shots of the pros just yet. Be content to get the ball onto the green.

1   Pitching wedge

2   9 iron

3   6 iron

6 iron

Pitching wedge

1 The high trajectory of the pitch shot reduces forward movement to a minimum.

2 The pitch and run has a lower trajectory and correspondingly more forward movement.

3 The chip shot has a low trajectory and produces maximum roll forwards towards the target.

repair it. This is part of the etiquette of the game.

The **chip** is usually played with a less lofted club, not one of the short irons. This time, the intention is not to loft the ball high into the air but only slightly, and then to get it to run on towards its target after landing.

Again you should adopt an open stance and shift more of your weight on to your left leg. Shorten the club by moving your hands down the handle and take some of the loft off the club by moving your hands forward a little bit.

Two of the finest exponents of chipping and pitching in the modern game are the Spaniards José-Maria Olazabal and Seve Ballesteros. Olazabal is a master at pitching while Ballesteros is a master at chipping. Watch how he makes full use of his knees when chipping, as does the top American golfer, Tom Watson.

9 iron

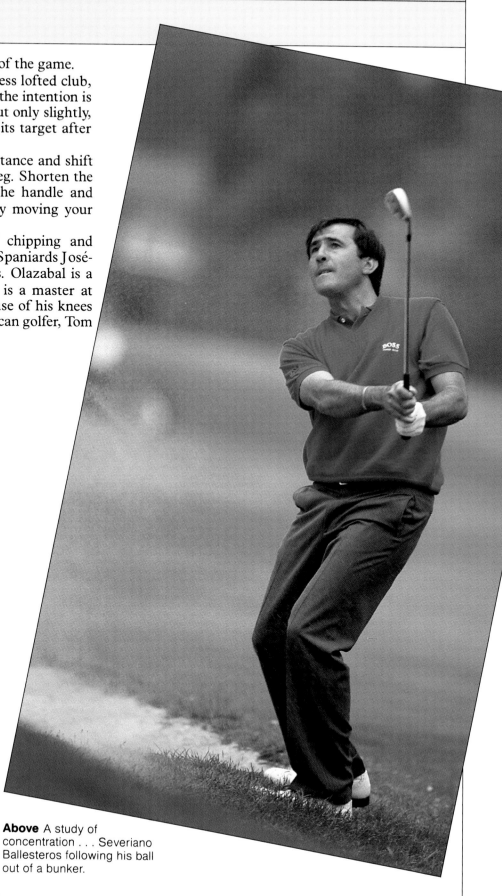

Above A study of concentration . . . Severiano Ballesteros following his ball out of a bunker.

GETTING OUT OF BUNKERS

WATCH THE LIKES of Gary Player, Paul Azinger, Scott Simpson and "Big Momma" JoAnne Carner, and getting out of bunkers seems like just another easy aspect of the game. But, in reality, the traps are so strategically placed that they should in some way handicap those wayward shots and certainly for the high-handicap player they do just that. But, once the fear of the bunker shot is overcome then landing in the sand should not prove too costly.

Player, Azinger, Simpson and Carner are all excellent sand players because they have one thing in common: they have spent hours practising the bunker shot, realizing how important it is to get out of the bunker cleanly and accurately. So, the first hint is *practice*. It is, perhaps, the one aspect of the game that the club player neglects. But it is just as important as driving, pitching, and putting.

There are two types of bunker: the **fairway bunker** and the **greenside bunker**. Let us look at the fairway bunker first.

The one thing you must remember when playing from a **fairway bunker** is not to be too ambitious.

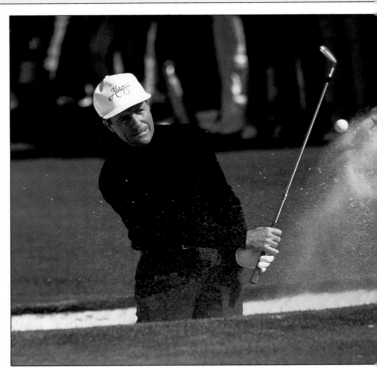

PLAYING OUT OF A GREENSIDE BUNKER

When playing out of greenside bunkers adopt a very open stance (A). Keep your eye fixed on the sand just behind the ball (B). Make contact with the area of sand you have fixed your eyes on (C). A correct contact will see the sand lift the ball out of the bunker (D).

A   B   C   D

Left Gary Player learned at an early stage in his career that it was crucial to be able to play good and accurate bunker shots and he spent hour after hour playing out of traps.

Right Britain's Laura Davies playing out of a bunker during the 1991 Women's Open.

OK, Fred Couples played a wonderful shot from a fairway bunker on his way to winning the 1992 US Masters. But he's Fred Couples. Your ball may be sitting up nicely and you think, "I can hit the green with a 4-iron". What happens next? Your confidence gets the better of you, the ball is not hit properly, it catches the lip of the bunker and back into the sand it rolls.

It is recommended that you take something between a 5- or 7-iron, or even a utility wood, like a 5- or 7-wood. Make sure your stance is square, and not an open one as when playing out of greenside bunkers. Focus your eyes on the back of the ball as normal but make sure you don't take sand first. Take the ball first.

Your ball may be so lodged in the bunker that it is impossible to come out forwards. In that case, remember what we said, don't be ambitious. If you have to play out sideways or backwards then do so. It may well be your best option. One thing to remember about bunker play is that you must *not* ground your club in the sand, and the first time the clubhead makes contact with the sand is when you play the shot. If you do ground it earlier you will be penalized two strokes in strokeplay and forfeit the hole in matchplay.

The approach to **greenside bunkers** is very different because you have very little room to work in, and you must get the ball out cleanly, but then get it to stop on the green.

Before you enter the bunker, weigh up your shot and get an idea of the distance you have to play. Once in the bunker get your feet comfortable and open your stance. Make sure the ball is level with your right heel. It is important this time when opening your stance that your shoulders should follow the same line as your stance and not remain square to the ball-to-target line. The leading edge of the club should, however, be square to the ball and ball-to-target line.

The backswing is mostly a wrist and arms action and is made along the line of your shoulders, not the ball-to-target line. Concentrate your eyes on the area of sand approximately 2in (5cm) behind the ball

because it is here that the clubhead is going to strike. It is *not going to strike the ball.* Because the club face is open, and you apply an "out-to-in" swing, it will travel under the ball and lift it out of the sand.

Before finishing with bunkers, there are two important etiquette rules that you should remember.
• Always enter the bunker from the back, not the front.
• After playing your shot rake over all your footprints.

DID YOU KNOW?

The word "caddie" comes from the French word "cadet". The first player to use a caddie or "cadet" is believed to be the Marquis of Montrose in the early 17th century.

PUTTING

HAVING DONE THE seemingly hard part and hit that little white ball the quarter of a mile from tee to green, it now comes down to the "simple" task of putting the ball into that hole. But how often is a potentially good score ruined by poor putting?

This part of the game must be practised more than any other because, don't forget, a saved shot on every putting green reduces your round by 18 strokes. That can make the difference between a round of 100 and one of 82. Doesn't 82 sound a lot better than 100?

When putting, everything you have learned about the basic golf swing must be forgotten because we are going to start afresh.

Firstly, you adopt a different hold. The most popular is the reverse overlap, but it is one of those areas where you have to adopt a hold that you feel comfortable and successful with. Firstly try the reverse overlap, and then modify it if you want to.

To achieve the reverse overlap, nine of your ten fingers (the index finger of your left hand being the exception) grip the club handle. All four fingers and thumb of the right hand grip the handle with the thumb resting on the flat part if there is one. The last three fingers and thumb of the left hand also grip the handle, again with the thumb resting on the flattened part. The other finger, the index finger, rests across the fingers of the right hand.

The putting stroke is not played with the wrists. They should remain uncocked as the stroke is made with the arms, shoulders and club acting as a single unit and moving accordingly.

Unlike the basic golf shot, your head should now be positioned directly over the ball, not behind it. But your head must remain still throughout the putting stroke.

The club face should be lined up square with the ball and target, with the ball lined up with the middle of the putter. There is usually a marker on top of the putter head to indicate the middle of the club face.

Position of the ball in relation to your feet at address is a personal thing. Most players have it lined up with their left toe, but when you look at the top professionals you will see a wide variety of putting actions. But all are effective, some more than others. Payne Stewart, for example, has a very upright putting stance with the toe of the putter on the ground and the heel off it. But he still sinks those putts!

It cannot be stressed too much that you should

PUTTING TECHNIQUE

In the correct putting hold (left), note how all the fingers, except the index finger of the left hand, hold the club. Even weight distribution between both feet is essential. To help achieve this ensure the outside edges of your shoes are level with your shoulders (below left). The putting stroke is an arms and shoulders movement only. The rest of the body should remain still (below right).

YOUR QUESTIONS ANSWERED

Q **What is meant by "reading" the greens?**

A Not all putting surfaces are perfectly flat and level, in fact very few are. All have some sort of undulations or individual peculiarity which must be identified before making a putt. There may be a roll from the left to the right, it may be an uphill putt, a downhill putt, and so on. You must walk around the green to establish this before attempting your putt. But once you have decided which way the green rolls, or whatever, you must make allowance for it with your putting stroke by aiming more to the left or right, or hitting it with more or less power. But you must remember that *all putts are straight*. It is the borrow of the green and speed the ball is hit which determine in which direction it travels. One good word of advice about putting: make your mind up about the putt and *don't change it*.

Q **What are the important things to remember when first putting out?**

A To begin with, the person furthest away from the hole always plays first. If the ball is on the putting surface the flag must be either out of the hole or tended, but it must be taken out as soon as the ball is played. Any person holding the flag must remain perfectly still during the putting stroke and all other playing members should remain still, quiet, and keep out of his line of sight while another player is putting.
Secondly, if your ball is just off the green then you can opt to have the flag out, left in, or tended. If you opt for it to be left in and the ball strikes it before entering the hole the stroke is perfectly legal.
Finally, a round of golf can take a long time to complete and there is nothing worse than having to wait while a match takes time to clear the green ahead, because they are marking their cards, or analysing putts. Get the putting over and done with and leave the green quickly for the next match. When you approach the putting area, note where the next hole is so that you can place your bags ready to move on.

spend time on the practice greens. That is what they are there for. And when putting don't be too ambitious. If you can get down in two putts on every hole then you are well on your way to becoming a low handicap player. Don't attack the hole with every shot. Imagine the hole as being six feet wide. If it was you would hole every putt in one. So, aim to get the ball into that six-foot hole, and if you manage that each time then you are left with an easier second putt. But it is those putts from about six feet that you should be practising.

The putting surfaces are carefully manicured and are the pride and joy of every greenkeeper. His skill in preparing the green must never be forgotten or abused. Therefore, there are some very important points to remember when on the putting surface.

Do not take golf trolleys onto the green and don't put your golf bag on the putting surface. Make sure your, and other unrepaired, pitch marks are repaired, and when you take the flag stick out of the hole, don't throw it onto the green; gently place it.

Bob Charles was one of the game's finest putters and was the most outstanding left-handed golfer. He captured the British Open title in 1963.

AWKWARD SHOTS

UPHILL AND DOWNHILL lies often catch the novice out but they are not as difficult as they seem, provided the necessary adjustments to the basic golf swing are made.

THE UPHILL LIE

When faced with an uphill lie the first thing you must do is set the body so that it is perpendicular to the ground. The ball should be further back in the address position than you would normally expect it with the same club. On the subject of clubs, because the ball will be "taking off" on the up slope, you will need to make allowances for this when selecting your club by taking a less lofted club.

A slight in-to-out swing path should be adopted. This will result in the ball being hooked slightly so aim marginally to the right of your intended target. Keep your head still throughout the shot.

THE DOWNHILL LIE

The downhill lie is much more difficult to play than the uphill lie. Again, your body must be set perpendicular to the ground. But, because you are leaning to the left, you must control your head and make sure it is still positioned behind the ball. It is not easy, but essential to the shot.

The ball should again be slightly back in the address position, and because of the position of the ball a more lofted club should be selected. This time an out-to-in swing path will probably be created so you therefore need to aim slightly to the left of the target to compensate for the slice.

PLAYING THE BALL BELOW YOUR FEET

Balance is the key word yet again. The tendency this time is to fall forward with your weight distribution moved to your toes. To compensate, bend your knees more than usual to maintain a good balance. Hold the club near the end of the handle and position the ball midway between your two feet at address. Aim marginally to the left of your target because the downswing will naturally create a shift of balance to your toes and an out-to-in swing path will result, thus creating a slice.

Top Playing the uphill lie. Note how important it is to keep the body perpendicular to the ground.

Above For a downhill lie the body should be kept perpendicular to the ground.

Above When playing the ball below your feet, bend your knees more than normal and aim slightly to the left of your target.

Above right Adopt a more upright stance when playing with the ball above your feet and this time aim to the right of your intended target.

PLAYING THE BALL ABOVE YOUR FEET

This time you have to shorten the club by holding it further down the handle. The ball should still, however, be positioned midway between your two feet but, because the flat swing created by your stance will create an in-to-out swing path, you must aim to the right of your intended target to compensate for the hook.

BALL AT THE FRONT OF A BUNKER

You must first realistically assess your chances of getting out of the bunker. Remember what we said about being over-ambitious. If there seems to be no way out at the front of the bunker then look at the options of playing out sideways or backwards.

However, if you do have a shot then you have to approach it in a different manner than you would playing a conventional shot from the bunker. Because of the ball's position you will be standing in a very difficult position, with one leg higher than the other, so it is important to maintain a good balance. Placing a lot of weight on to your left leg will help with your balance. You should make sure your stance is very open.

BALL AT THE BACK OF A BUNKER

A ball positioned close to the back of the bunker generally poses more problems because you may have to play the shot standing outside the bunker. No matter whether you are standing in or out of the bunker you must create a very upright backswing to

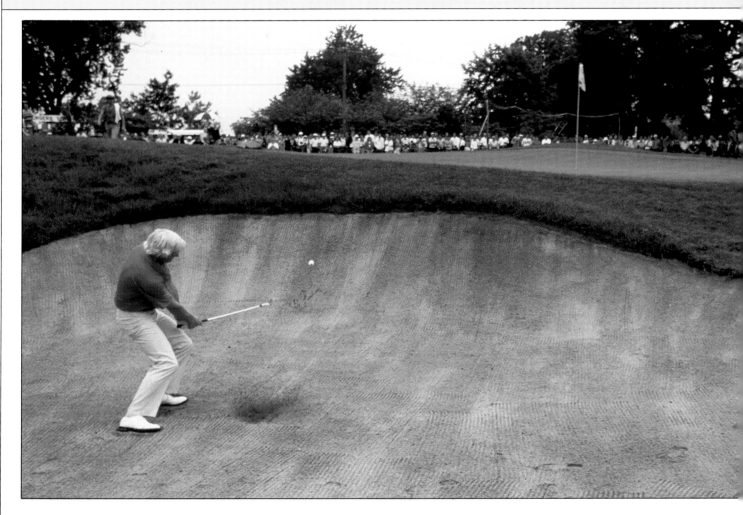

prevent catching the edge of the bunker with the clubhead. The upright swing will open the club face at impact and it is important that you follow through correctly.

BALL PLUGGED IN A BUNKER

Adopt a square stance, not an open one, and have the ball positioned midway between your two feet. Make sure the clubhead is closed and blast the ball out of the sand. The soft sand will cause the closed face to open on impact. Make sure you follow through after impact - if you can!

PLAYING OUT OF THE ROUGH

The rough is that uncut area on either side of the fairway. The rough on the fringe of the fairway is often not as severe as that beyond it and is known as the light rough. Quite often it is easy to play out of the light rough and it may have little or no difference to the outcome of your score on the hole. If the ball is "sitting up" then there is no reason why you shouldn't take a wooden club out of the light rough.

If it is "sitting up" it is resting on top of the rough, which is longer than the fairway grass. Therefore, when you adopt your stance your feet will be firmly on the ground and your ball will be higher than normal. So, to compensate for this and prevent your clubhead passing directly underneath the ball, you should shorten the club by moving your hands down the handle and then play the shot in the normal way.

The long grass, or deep rough, poses more problems and it is here that we again use that word "ambition". Perhaps you would be better taking a 9-iron and pitching back onto the fairway? Don't forget, if you are in big trouble in the deep rough it is because you played a bad shot in the first place.

Left Bunkers like this are a daunting prospect for the club player, but to Australia's Greg Norman one of the Winged Foot 'monsters' poses no problem.

Below right Severiano Ballesteros is the master of the recovery shot and it is no problem for him to recover from long rough like this.

DID YOU KNOW?

Some long-standing golf superstitions maintain that it was bad luck to enter the clubhouse and find a black cat sleeping on your golf bag; to stumble on the steps leading from the fourth tee; to have a robin alight on the iron marker of the hole you're approaching; to leave your pencil in the locker and have to borrow one from your opponent.

What makes you think that you are now capable of following it with a superhuman shot as a means of recovery? Come on! Leave that to the likes of Seve Ballesteros.

Again, your lie will dictate which club you use, but you are recommended to take a club with a heavier head, like a 9-iron or wedge. The reason for this is because the clubhead will likely get entangled in the long grass and the heavier clubhead will help overcome this to a certain extent. Remember that a utility wood, 5- or 7-wood will be heavy enough in many cases to get your ball out of deep rough without getting the shaft tangled in the grass or whatever.

It is important that you attack the ball with an upright backswing which will again help prevent the club getting entangled in the grass. Mind you, if you are in the deep rough, you may be surrounded by trees, bushes, and so on, and they will all dictate what kind of backswing you have.

You can only learn a certain amount about this wonderful, if at times frustrating, game from a book. The rest is up to you. Mental attitude, and the ability and desire to practise, will only make you a better player. And you are well advised to have a few lessons with a PGA professional before you pick up too many bad habits.

GOLF GREATS

THE WORLD OF golf has provided many great
personalities, probably more than any other sport.
They have spanned many eras, starting from the early
days of championship golf back in 1860. GREAT
PLAYERS is a selection of some of those greats whose
names will always be part of golfing lore.

A Tour is a season-long series of events which sees
the best golfers, whether they be male, female, or
senior players, competing for much sought-after
prize money. GREAT TOURS takes us round the world
with some of the most exciting players ever.

All the world's leading golfers regularly compete
against each other but during the year they gather
specially for the likes of the British and US Open,
Masters, PGA Championship
and so on. The GREAT
TOURNAMENTS gives an
insight into these
top-class and very
exciting events.

GREAT PLAYERS: MEN

SEVERIANO BALLESTEROS
(Spain, born 1957)
Ballesteros first attracted attention when he finished joint second in the 1976 British Open at the age of 19. He then went on to win the Open in 1979 and the following year became the youngest winner of the US Masters. He has won more than 50 events on the European Tour and his worldwide career earnings are in excess of £3 million.
Majors (5): *British Open 1979, 1984, 1988; US Masters 1980, 1983*

JAMES BRAID
(Great Britain, born 1870, died 1950)
Along with Harry Vardon and J H Taylor, James Braid was one of the Great Triumvirate that dominated British golf at the turn of the century, when they won the British Open 16 times between them. In later life Braid was a much respected golf course designer.
Majors (5): *British Open 1901, 1905-06, 1908, 1910*

Right James Braid.

Below The 'Great Triumvirate' of J H Taylor (stood right) James Braid (seated left) and Harry Vardon (seated right) are joined by another turn of the century great Sandy Herd.

Seve Ballesteros

BILLY CASPER
(United States, born 1931)
Billy Casper's record of 51 US Tour wins puts him sixth on the all-time list with only the game's greatest names in front of him. A member of eight Ryder Cup teams he has three Majors to his credit, and after joining the US Seniors Tour in 1981 he continued adding to his tally of successes.
Majors (3): *US Open 1959, 1966; US Masters 1970*

HENRY COTTON
(Great Britain, born 1907, died 1987)
Britain's finest golfer in the 1930s and 40s, Henry Cotton is the only man to win the British Open both before and after World War II. When he won his first Open at Sandwich in 1934 he did so with a round of 65, which was to remain unbeaten until 1977.
Majors (3): *British Open 1934, 1937, 1948*

Henry Cotton

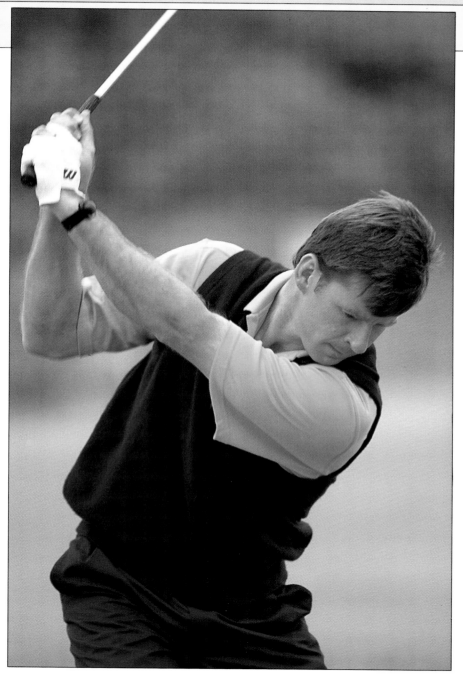

Nick Faldo

NICK FALDO
(Great Britain, born 1957)
In recent years the British have dominated world golf and none more so than Nick Faldo, who has taken on and beaten the Americans on home soil. He has won the British Open three times, and in 1990 became only the second man after Jack Nicklaus to retain the US Masters title. His career earnings have soared beyond the £2.5 million mark.
Majors (5): *British Open 1987, 1990, 1992; US Masters 1989-90*

WALTER HAGEN
(United States, born 1892, died 1969)
The flamboyant Walter Hagen takes a lot of credit for obtaining the recognition the professional

Walter Hagen

BOBBY JONES
(United States, born 1902, died 1971)
Without question Bobby Jones was the world's greatest amateur player. And such was his record that he was a match for any of the day's professionals, including Walter Hagen. In 1930 Jones achieved the greatest grand slam in golf when he won the amateur and Open titles of *both* the United States and Great Britain.
Majors (7): *British Open 1926-27, 1930; US Open 1923, 1926, 1929- 30*

TOM KITE
(United States, born 1949)
The biggest money winner in US golf history, Tom Kite looked like being stuck with the tag "the best man never to win a major", until 1992 when he captured the US Open. Two years earlier he became the first man to win more than $6 million on the US tour. Texas-born

Tom Kite

golfers of today now receive. He identified himself with the ordinary man and broke down the myth that golf was played by a select few. He was a great character; furthermore he was a great golfer and was one of the finest matchplay exponents in the 1920s.
Majors (11): *British Open 1922, 1924, 1928-29; US Open 1914, 1919; US PGA 1921, 1924-27*

BEN HOGAN
(United States, born 1912)
The golf world was dominated by three men from the late 1930s to

40s: Sam Snead, Byron Nelson and Ben Hogan. And it was Hogan's stylish play that kept him at the top for more than a decade. He is best remembered for his courageous comeback following a road accident in 1949. He went on to win the US Open the following year after being told he would never walk again. In 1953 he won three Majors, something no other man has done in one year.
Majors (9): *British Open 1953; US Open 1948, 1950-51, 1953; US Masters 1951, 1953; US PGA 1946, 1948*

Tom Kite was runner-up to Larry Wadkins in the 1970 US Amateur Championship and turned professional two years later.
Majors (1): *US Open 1992*

BOBBY LOCKE
(South Africa, born 1917, died 1987)
South Africa's first great golfer was Bobby Locke who, along with Australia's Peter Thomson, dominated the British Open in the 1950s. Famous for his plus fours and white cap, Locke won more than 80 tournaments worldwide, including several on the US circuit in the early post-war years.
Majors (4): *British Open 1949-50, 1952, 1957*

Bobby Locke

TOM MORRIS, JNR
(Great Britain, born 1851, died 1875)
Young Tom Morris is probably the finest golfer that ever lived. A professional at the age of 14, he won his first British Open when only 17 and by the age of 20 he had won four titles. He is the only man to win four successive titles (there was no competition in 1871). His total would have been more had he not died at the age of 24 following a bout of depression after his wife and newborn baby had died in childbirth.
Majors (4): *British Open 1868-70, 1872*

TOM MORRIS, SNR
(Great Britain, born 1821, died 1908)
The first of the greats of Championship golf, Old Tom Morris, like his son, won four British Open titles. He was also a

Old Tom Morris (left) and his son, Young Tommy

great match player and along with another great of the game, Allan Robertson, they formed an invincible team. Morris started his career as an apprentice ball-maker with Robertson.

Majors (4): *British Open 1861-62, 1864, 1867*

BYRON NELSON
(United States, born 1912)
Nelson holds a place in golfing history because, in 1945, he won a US Tour record 18 events in one season, including a staggering 11 consecutively. At the peak of his career he went 113 tournaments without missing the cut and his total of 52 US Tour wins puts him fifth on the all-time list.
Majors (5): *US Open 1939; US Masters 1937, 1942; US PGA 1940, 1945*

JACK NICKLAUS
(United States, born 1940)
Jack Nicklaus is unquestionably the finest golfer of the modern era and his record of 18 professional Majors is seven more than the next best man, Walter Hagen. Nicklaus achieved his victories at a time

Byron Nelson

Jack Nicklaus

when the golf world was littered with many talented players thus making his achievement even more outstanding. The US Amateur champion in 1959 and 1961, he made a name for himself in the 1960 US Open when he pushed Arnold Palmer all the way before losing by two strokes. The "Master" of Augusta, Nicklaus has won the Masters a record six times, including 1986 when he was 46 years of age. Since joining the Seniors Tour he has continued his winning ways.
Majors (18): *British Open 1966, 1970, 1978; US Open 1962, 1967, 1972, 1980; US Masters 1963, 1965-66, 1972, 1975, 1986; US PGA 1963, 1971, 1973, 1975, 1980*

GREG NORMAN
(Australia, born 1955)
Greg Norman burst onto the international scene in 1980 when he captured the French Open,

Australian Open, Scandinavian Open and World Matchplay championship at Wentworth. He has since won many other tournaments in his homeland, Europe and in the United States where he has twice been the top money-winner. However, he still has just one Major to his credit, even though he came close to capturing all four in 1986, a feat so far not achieved. He led all four championships going into the final round only to see three titles taken away from him. The only one he captured was the British Open.
Major (1): *British Open 1986*

FRANCIS OUIMET
(United States, born 1893, died 1967)
This amateur changed the whole face of world golf when he took on and beat two of Britain's best

Francis Ouimet (centre) with Harry Vardon (left) and Ted Ray (right), 1913

Arnold Palmer

owed a huge debt by his fellow professionals and the golf world in general. On top of all that, Arnold Palmer was a very good golfer and remains one of the world's best-loved players.

Majors (7): *British Open 1961-62: US Open 1960; US Masters 1958, 1960, 1962, 1964*

GARY PLAYER
(South Africa, born 1935)
Along with Arnold Palmer and Jack Nicklaus, South Africa's Gary Player helped popularize golf in the 1960s and for more than 30 years he has been delighting golf fans the world over. He has uniquely won the British Open in three post-war decades and his 22 wins on US soil is a record for a non-American.

Majors (9): *British Open 1959, 1968, 1974; US Open 1965; US Masters 1961, 1974, 1978; US PGA 1962, 1972*

Gary Player

professionals, Harry Vardon and Ted Ray, by five and six strokes, to win the play-off and take the US Open at Brookline, Massachusetts in 1913. His victory opened the door for American golf and his countrymen have never looked back. Ouimet won the US Amateur title twice, in 1914 and 1931.

Major (1): *US Open 1913*

ARNOLD PALMER
(United States, born 1929)
Arnold Palmer is the man who popularized golf in the 1960s. Furthermore, he was responsible for ensuring the British Open maintained its standing as the world's foremost tournament, because he made sure his fellow Americans continued to make the trip across the Atlantic each year. Palmer, along with his business partner, Mark McCormack, also improved standards and earnings for the professional golfer. He is

Allan Robertson

ALLAN ROBERTSON
(Great Britain, born 1815, died 1859)
The name of Allan Robertson may not be a familiar one, but he was probably the first real great of golf in the pre-tournament days. And it was upon his death that a tournament, the British Open, was inaugurated to find his "successor". As a match player, Robertson was unbeatable and it is said that he never lost a fourball match.

GENE SARAZEN
(United States, born 1902)
Eugene Sarazen may have won seven Majors during his career but he will always be remembered for two of golf's most memorable

Sam Snead

shots. The first was on his way to winning his only Masters title in 1935 when he holed a 220-yard four wood shot at the par-5 15th for a double eagle two. Thirty-eight years later at Troon, Sarazen holed the Postage Stamp (8th) in one during the British Open. His achievement was caught on camera to add to the glamour of the occasion.

Majors (7): *US Open 1922, 1932; British Open 1932; US Masters 1935; US PGA 1922-23, 1933*

SAM SNEAD
(United States, born 1912)
Sam Snead has won more US Tour events than any other man. His total of 81 is 11 more than second-placed Jack Nicklaus, but unlike Nicklaus, Snead never captured

the top prize in US golf, the Open, although he was four times runner-up. When he won the 1965 Greater Greensboro Open he became, at 52, the oldest winner on the US Tour. And in 1979 he shot his own age in the Quad Cities Tournament.

Majors (7): *British Open 1946; US Masters 1949, 1952, 1954; US PGA 1942, 1949, 1951*

JOHN HENRY "J H" TAYLOR
(Great Britain, born 1871, died 1963)
Another of the Great Triumvirate along with Harry Vardon and James Braid, J H won five British Open titles. He turned professional at the age of 19 and later in life was largely responsible for the formation of the PGA as he sought to improve the professional's lot.

Majors (5): *British Open 1894-95, 1900, 1909, 1913*

PETER THOMSON
(Australia, born 1929)
Australian golf is enjoying a tremendous upsurge in the 1990s, but the man who started it all was Peter Thomson in the 1950s. He won a modern-day record-equalling five British Opens, including three in succession, and in seven consecutive years 1952-58 he never finished lower than second. He was made an honorary member of the R & A in 1982.

Majors (5): *British Open 1954-56, 1958, 1965*

LEE TREVINO
(United States, born 1939)
Every sport needs its characters and there is none greater in the world of golf than Lee Trevino. He makes the game fun; he also makes it look easy and his record of 27 US Tour wins and career winnings in excess of $3 million

confirm him as one of the all-time greats of the game. In 1971 he achieved a remarkable hat-trick by winning the US, Canadian and British Open titles within three weeks of each other.

Majors (6): *British Open 1971-72; US Open 1968, 1971; US PGA 1974, 1984*

HARRY VARDON
(Great Britain, born 1870, died 1937)
Jersey-born Harry Vardon was the most successful of golf's Great Triumvirate, winning the British Open a record six times. And his victory in 1914 completed the run of 16 Open wins in 20 years by Messrs Braid, Taylor and Vardon. He also won the US Open in 1900

Lee Trevino

Peter Thomson

Tom Watson

<table>
</table>

It is a little known fact that
Peter Alliss, who became a
professional golfer at the
age of 15, has written
a novel called
The Duke.

DID YOU KNOW?

and his victory helped spark off a
great deal of interest in the game
in America.

Majors (7): *British Open 1896,
1898-99, 1903, 1911, 1914; US
Open 1900*

TOM WATSON
(United States, born 1949)
With 32 US Tour wins, over $5
million career winnings and five
British Opens to his credit, Tom
Watson is rightly amongst the list
of all-time best golfers. His British
Open record is a remarkable
modern-day achievement and the
way he is still playing, his
equalling of Harry Vardon's record
cannot be ruled out.

Majors (8): *British Open 1975,
1977, 1980, 1982-83; US Open
1982; US Masters 1977, 1981*

GREAT PLAYERS: WOMEN

PATTY BERG
(United States, born 1918)
A teenage prodigy, Patty Berg gained recognition by reaching the final of the US Amateur as a 17-year-old. She turned professional in 1940 and it was off the golf course, as the first president of the US LPGA, that she became acknowledged as one of the game's outstanding female figures.
Major victories: *US Amateur 1938; US Open 1946; World Champion 1953-55, 1957*

JOANNE CARNER (née GUNDERSON)
(United States, born 1939)
Known as "Big Momma", JoAnne

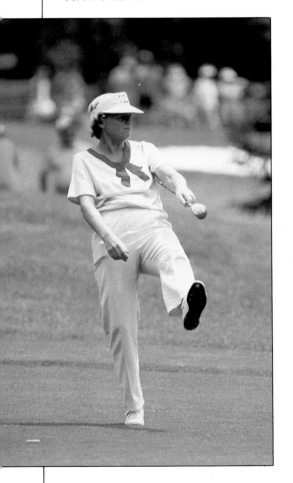

JoAnne Carner

Carner has been thrilling US crowds for more than 30 years and in 1987, at the age of 48, she came close to winning the US Open, but lost a three-way play-off which Britain's Laura Davies won. JoAnne won her first of five Amateur titles at the age of 18. She did not turn professional until she was 30.
Major victories: *US Amateur 1957, 1960, 1962, 1966, 1968; US Open 1971, 1976*

SANDRA HAYNIE
(United States, born 1943)
Birdies at the last two holes enabled Sandra Haynie to capture her first US Open in 1974 by one stroke. She has won four women's Majors, capturing the LPGA title twice, the Open once and the Du Maurier Classic once. She joined the US Tour in 1961 and was the top Tour winner in 1974 and 1975 with 10 victories.
Major victories: *US Open 1974; US LPGA 1965, 1974; Du Maurier Classic 1982*

BETTY JAMESON
(United States, born 1919)
After a successful amateur career that yielded two Amateur titles, Betty Jameson became one of the pioneers of the women's professional game in the post-war years. She was runner-up in the first US Open in 1946 but came back to win the following year by six strokes. She retired in 1965.
Major victories: *US Open 1947; US Amateur 1939-40*

CATHERINE LACOSTE
(France, born 1945)
One of France's leading lady golfers, Catherine Lacoste became the first amateur, and first non-American, to win the US Women's Open when she won at Hot

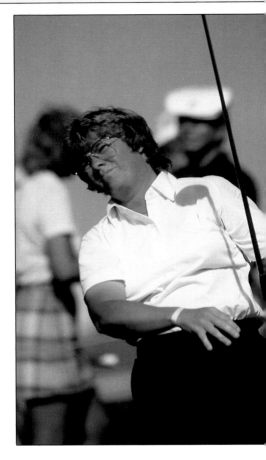

Sandra Haynie

Springs, Virginia, in 1967. She also became the youngest ever winner. Two years later she completed a notable double by winning the amateur titles of America and Britain in the same year. Catherine Lacoste came from a sporting family. Her father was tennis player René Lacoste, one of the famous French *Four Musketeers*, and her mother, Thion de la Chaume, won the British Open Ladies' Golf title in 1927. Catherine Lacoste was a member of France's World Amateur championship-winning team in 1964.
Major victories: *US Open 1967; US Amateur 1969; British Amateur 1969*

CECILIA LEITCH
(Great Britain, born 1891, died 1977)
Known as Cecil, she won a record four British Amateur titles between 1914 and 1926 and remarkably each of her four victories came in a different one of the four home countries. She had made her debut in the championship in 1908, her first serious competition, and she introduced to the game power and mastery of woods not previously seen in the women's game. In addition to winning titles in Britain, Cecilia Leitch captured five French Open titles and in 1921 had a remarkable 17 and 15 win to take the Canadian Open.
Major victories: *British Amateur 1914, 1920-21, 1926; English Ladies 1914, 1919*

NANCY LOPEZ
(United States, born 1957)
Nancy Lopez made an immediate impact in her debut season as a professional by finishing second in the US Open. She has gone on to confirm that early promise and become one of the biggest money winners on the US Tour with over $3 million. After winning her 35th Tour event in 1987 she was inducted into the Hall of Fame.
Major victories: *US LPGA 1978, 1985, 1989*

CAROL MANN
(United States, born 1941)
In winning the 1965 US Open, 6ft 3in tall Carol Mann showed great determination to come back after shooting an opening-round 78 and

Left Nancy Lopez

Below Carol Mann

Above Joyce Wethered

Left Louise Suggs

make up a seven-stroke deficit. A member of the ladies tour since 1961 she was top money-winner in 1969 and has enjoyed nearly 40 Tour wins, including eight in her top money-making season.
Major victory: *US Open 1965*

BETSY RAWLS
(United States, born 1928)
One of the early greats of the ladies professional tour, Betsy Rawls won the first of four US Opens in her debut season as a professional in 1951. The previous year she was runner-up as an amateur. The leading money winner in 1952 and 1959, she

ended her career with 55 Tour wins. She later became president and then tournament director of the LPGA.
Major victories: *US Open 1951, 1953, 1957, 1960; US LPGA 1959, 1969*

LOUISE SUGGS
(United States, born 1923)
After a very successful amateur career which saw her win the US and British amateur titles in successive years, Louise Suggs turned professional and vindicated her decision by winning all the major honours the game could offer. In addition to winning the

US Open twice she was runner-up no less than five times. Her efforts for improving the lady professionals' standing was rewarded with her appointment as president of the LPGA in 1956. She won 50 Tour events.
Major victories: *US Open 1949, 1952; US LPGA 1957; US Amateur 1947; British Amateur 1948*

GLENNA VARE (née COLLETT)
(United States, born 1903)
A great favourite with galleries and fellow professionals, Glenna Collett's record of six US Amateur titles, including three in

succession, is likely to remain unbeaten for a long time. Captain of the US Curtis Cup team four times.
Major victories: *US Amateur 1922, 1925, 1928-30, 1935*

JOYCE WETHERED
(Great Britain, born 1901)
Joyce Wethered won five consecutive English championships and four of the six British championships she entered.

Kathy Whitworth

A student of Harry Vardon and J H Taylor in her early days, the great Bobby Jones once described her swing as "one of the best ever" by man or woman. Indeed a great compliment for one of Britain's best-ever lady golfers. She became Lady Heathcoate-Amory after marrying Sir John Amory.
Major victories: *British Open 1922, 1924-25, 1929; English Championship 1920-24*

KATHY WHITWORTH
(United States, born 1939)
The most successful golfer on the US Women's Tour with 88 wins. Like her male counterpart, Sam Snead, she too has never won the US Open, although she has captured six women's Majors. Kathy Whitworth carried on where Mickey Wright left off and became the sport's premier lady throughout the 60s and 70s.
Major victories: *US LPGA 1967, 1971, 1975*

MICKEY WRIGHT
(United States, born 1935)
Mickey Wright's 82 Tour wins are second only to Kathy Whitworth's all-time record of 88. She was invincible in the 1960s and was top money winner four years in succession from 1961 to 1964, during which time she won 44 tournaments including a record 13 in 1963. She had great power and her presence considerably improved the standard of the women's game. Her total of 12 Majors is a women's record.
Major victories: *US Open 1958-59, 1961, 1964; US PGA 1958, 1960-61, 1963*

MILDRED "BABE" ZAHARIAS (née DIDRIKSON)
(United States, born 1915, died 1956)

Babe Zaharias

Mildred acquired the name "Babe" after her baseball idol Babe Ruth. An all-round sportswoman she won two track and field gold medals at the 1932 Olympics before turning to golf. She became equally successful at her new sport and after winning the 1946 US Amateur title she became the first American to win the British title a year later. She then turned professional and in 1948 won the US Open. She was top money winner in the LPGA Tour's first four years, when she registered 19 of her 31 Tour wins. She lost her fight against cancer in 1956.
Major victories: *US Open 1948, 1950, 1954; US Amateur 1946; British Amateur 1947*

US PGA TOUR

THE US TOUR effectively started with the launch of the US Open in 1895, and four years later when the Western Open was first played it became a "two-event tour". But the forerunner of the modern-day Tour started back in the 1920s, when club professionals from all over America would meet in the winter months to play a series of competitions in the warmer southern states, starting on the West Coast and moving around to the East Coast by spring before eventually returning to their club jobs for the summer months.

With the likes of Walter Hagen, Bobby Jones and Gene Sarazen joining the Tour it became very popular, and by the end of the decade the Los Angeles Open, Pensacola Open, Texas Open and Western Open were all regular annual fixtures. The Western Open, dating to 1899, is the oldest event on the US calendar after the US Open.

Other tournaments became regular fixtures in the 1930s. There were the Bing Crosby Pro-Am, Phoenix Open Invitational, Greater New Orleans Open Invitational and Greater Greensboro Open.

Despite a financial decline in the United States, the golf Tour still continued to attract large galleries during the 1930s as it continued to grow in popularity with both players and spectators alike. And it was during this period that some of the next generation of leading American golfers were spawned including Sam Snead, Byron Nelson and Ben Hogan.

After World War II the Tour became more structured and organized. Prize money increased and the Tour developed rapidly when television became a regular "spectator". Sponsors were

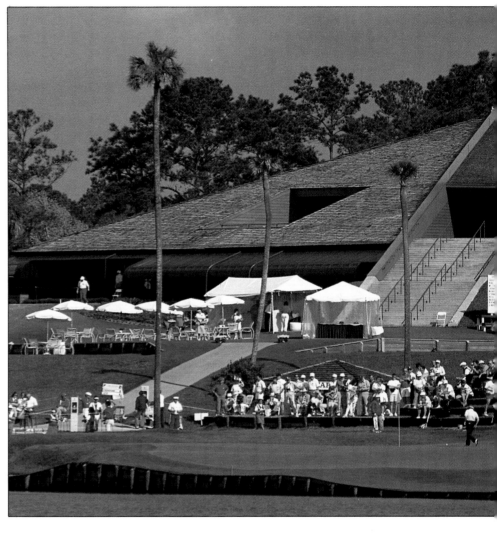

queuing up to be associated with individual events and this revenue, together with television rights, resulted in purses soaring.

The touring professionals took over the control of the events in 1968 when they formed the Tournament Players Division.

Prize money on offer today exceeds $50 million per season. But the money doesn't all go to the professionals. The PGA Tour is proud of its slogan which says: "The leading money winner on the US PGA TOUR is Charity," because, since 1984, it has donated more than $100 million to various charities.

Action from the 1988 Players Championship, won by Mark McCumber. The Championship is played at the US PGA Tour's headquarters at Sawgrass, Ponte Vedra, Florida.

Such is the demand to join the Tour that a satellite tour was established, and players finishing outside the top 125 on the money list each season have to compete in an end-of-season "school", along with other aspirants, to regain or gain their ticket to play on the Tour.

US PGA TOUR RECORDS AND MILESTONES

Records
Most tournament wins:	81 Sam Snead (1936-65)
Most wins in one year:	18 Byron Nelson (1945)
Most consecutive wins:	11 Byron Nelson (March-August 1945)
Most money won in a career:	$6,655,474 Tom Kite (1972-91)
Lowest 72-hole score:	257 Mike Souchak (1955 Texas Open)
Lowest 18-hole score:	59 Al Geiberger (1977 Memphis Classic)
	59 Chip Beck (1991 Las Vegas Invitational)
Oldest winner:	52 yrs 10 mths Sam Snead (1965 Greensboro Open)
Youngest winner:	19 yrs 10 mths Johnny McDermott (1911 US Open)
Most times top money winner:	8 Jack Nicklaus (1964-65, 1967, 1971-73, 1975-76)
Most money won in season	$1,395,278 Tom Kite (1989)

Milestones
Career
First player to win $1 million:	Arnold Palmer (21 Jul 1968)
First player to win $2 million:	Jack Nicklaus (1 Dec 1973)
First player to win $3 million:	Jack Nicklaus (22 May 1977)
First player to win $4 million:	Jack Nicklaus (6 Feb 1983)
First player to win $5 million:	Jack Nicklaus (20 Aug 1988)
First player to win $6 million:	Tom Kite (5 Aug 1990)

Season
First player to win $100,000:	Arnold Palmer (1963)
First player to win $250,000:	Jack Nicklaus (1972)
First player to win $500,000:	Tom Watson (1980)
First player to win $750,000:	Curtis Strange (1987)
First player to win $1 million:	Curtis Strange (1988)

DID YOU KNOW?

On 6 February 1971, astronaut Alan B Shepherd Jr hit a golf ball 200 yards (183m) on the moon, making golf the first sport to be played in outer space and maybe paving the way for a future intergalactic tour!

Above Deane R Beman, the US PGA Tour Commissioner was a first class golfer and twice won the US amateur title before turning professional.

Left A great golf fan and supporter of the US Tour, comedian Bob Hope.

THE EUROPEAN PGA TOUR

THE EUROPEAN PGA Tour, now known as the Volvo Tour, because of its sponsorship package with the Swedish car manufacturer, is the European equivalent of the US Tour, and each week 128 top professionals make their way across Europe in search of the £16 million prize money on offer during an eight-month season.

Like their American counterparts, British and European players have been competing together regularly in a series of events across Europe for many years, although most events were based in the British Isles.

The Tour as such really got under way in 1971, when John Jacobs was appointed by the PGA to make tournament play more financially viable and to organize

it on a business level. In his first year prize money was £250,000. Within four years he had doubled it. It was at that time that the Tournament Players separated themselves from the PGA and in 1977 they merged with the Continental Tournament Players' Association to form the European Players' Division.

Prize money was then up to around £700,000, but the interest shown by BBC television, and the Tour's decision to switch events to

Right The Wentworth clubhouse. The Surrey course has been the home of the World Matchplay Championship since its launch in 1964.

Below Action from the Volvo Tour.

a Sunday finish to fit into television schedules, proved to be the correct one and in 1978 total prize money exceeded £1 million. Today, it is up to £16 million, and the number of tournaments has more than doubled from 17 in 1975.

On 25 May 1987 the Tour signed a deal with Volvo, who became their first corporate sponsor, and from that date the Tour became known as the Volvo Tour.

Like the American Tour, the European PGA Tour has its own Qualifying School each autumn for all those players finishing outside the top 128 in the annual money list.

Nick Faldo, one of the top money winners on the European Tour, is seen teeing off at the 12th during the 1990 Volvo PGA Championship. However, it wasn't Faldo's year because victory went to Australia's Mike Harwood.

EUROPEAN PGA TOUR RECORDS AND MILESTONES

Records

Most tournament wins:	49 Severiano Ballesteros (1976-91)
Most wins in one year:	7 Norman von Nida (1947)
	7 Flory van Donck (1953)
Most consecutive wins:	4 Alf Padgham (1935-36)
	4 Severiano Ballesteros (1986)
Most money win in a career:	£2,691,090 Severiano Ballesteros
Lowest 72-hole score:	258 David Llewellyn (1988 AGF Biarritz Open)
	258 Ian Woosnam (1990 Torres Monte Carlo Open)
Lowest 18-hole score:	60 Baldovino Dassu (1971 Swiss Open)
	60 David Llewellyn (1988 AGF Biarritz Open)
	60 Ian Woosnam (1990 Torres Monte Carlo Open)
Oldest winner:	58 yrs Alex Herd (1926 *News of the World* Matchplay)
Youngest winner:	19 yrs 4 mths Severiano Ballesteros (1976 Dutch Open)
Most times top money winner:	6 Severiano Ballesteros (1976-78, 1986, 1988, 1991)
Most money won in season:	£737,977 Ian Woosnam (1990)

Milestones

Season

First player to win £25,000:	Christy O'Connor (1970)
First player to win £50,000:	Severiano Ballesteros (1978)
First player to win £100,000:	Nick Faldo (1983)
First player to win £250,000:	Severiano Ballesteros (1986)
First player to win £500,000:	Severiano Ballesteros (1988)

OTHER TOURS

THE SAFARI TOUR is organized by the European PGA Tour and is held in the months leading up to the start of that Tour. Players make their way to the Central and Western African nations to compete in a mini 5-event tour normally taking in Zimbabwe, Zambia, Kenya, Nigeria and the Ivory Coast. It is popular with many of the European Tour players who are keen to prepare themselves for the forthcoming season in Europe.

The Safari Tour was launched in the mid-1970s and the oldest of the five Opens is the Kenyan Open, which was launched in 1967. Sandy Lyle won his first major event when he captured the 1978 Nigerian Open, and his total of 124 for the first 36 holes is the lowest by any British professional. In the pro-am preceding the same event in 1973 David Jagger shot a world record-equalling 59.

The **Asian Tour** has gained in popularity in recent years as the Far East has become one of the biggest growth areas for golf, particularly in Japan. Consequently, large sums of money are being invested and leading professionals are lured to the country each year. The growth of the sport in Japan is highlighted by the fact that Tommy Nakajima, the Ozaki brothers, and the lady golfer Ayoka Okamoto have all become world-class competitors in recent years.

The Asian Tour started life as the Far East Tour in 1959 when Eric Cremin, an Australian professional, and Kim Hall, a Welshman, organized the Hong Kong Open. It was on this foundation that the Tour was truly established in 1961 when the Philippine and Singapore Opens were added.

Top One of Japan's leading players, Tsuneyuki 'Tommy' Nakajima (left) Another Japanese golfer, Ayoka Okamoto (right)

Above The Ozaki Brothers, Joe (left) and 'Jumbo' (right)

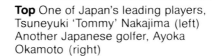

However, following the formation of the Asian Golf Confederation in 1963, the Tour blossomed but it has only been in the last decade, since the leading American and European golfers showed interest in the Tour, that it has snowballed and is one of the wealthiest Tours outside America.

Following the phenomenal growth of the sport in the country, the Japanese Tour was born separately out of the Asian Tour and the large purses attract many top golfers to Japan each year.

The **Australasian Tour** has been responsible for providing such wonderfully talented players as Ian Baker-Finch, Rodger Davis, Greg Norman, Craig Parry, Mike Harwood and so on in the 1980s as Australia has emerged as one of the world's leading nations.

Because it is held during the US and European Tours' winter months, it gives the opportunity for the professional golfer to play all the year round if he wishes. The three major events of the Tour are the New Zealand Open and the Australian Open and Masters.

South Africa has always produced fine golfers. Firstly there was Bobby Locke and then Gary Player. And in recent years there has been a spate of other talented golfers, all of whom used the **Sunshine Tour** as their training ground.

Like the Australasian Tour, it is held during the US and European Tours' winter months, thus offering more competitive play to the world's top players in the southern hemisphere. The highlight of the South African season is the million dollar challenge at Sun City every December, when invited players compete for the sport's richest prize.

Above The beautiful setting at Sun City, South Africa.

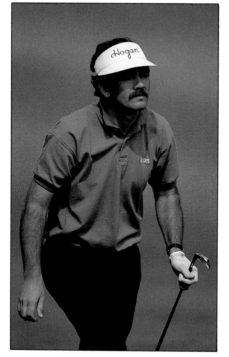

Above One of the current South African stars, David Frost.

Right Zimbabwe's Mark McNulty.

Right Now playing on the US Seniors Tour, Arnold Palmer remains as popular as ever and still attracts his 'army' of fans.

Facing page (top) Marie-Laure de Lorenzi of France in action during the Weetabix British Open.

Facing page (below) Pat Bradley, the first woman to win over $4 million on the US Women's Tour.

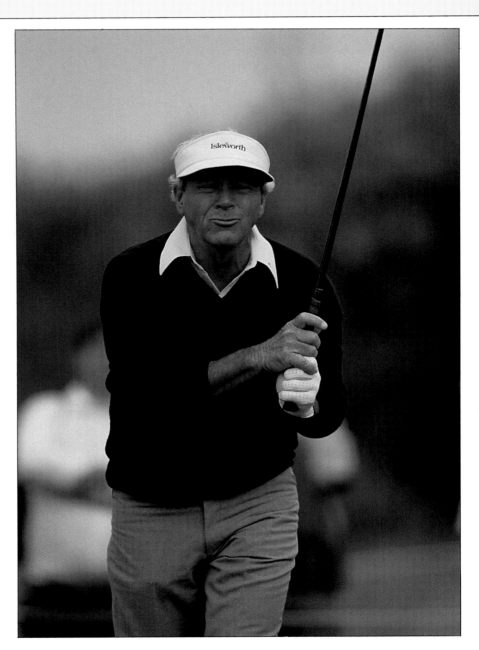

Back in the United States there is the very popular **PGA Seniors Tour** which is open to players upon reaching their 50th birthday and now, with Arnold Palmer, Jack Nicklaus, Gary Player and Lee Trevino beyond their 50th birthday, the interest in the Tour is greater than ever as such nostalgic memories are revived. The likes of Trevino and Nicklaus are winning more today on this Tour than they used to on the regular Tour. And in 1991 the top money winner on the Seniors Tour, Mike Hill, won more than Corey Pavin, the top money winner on the regular Tour. Hill won in excess of $1 million.

And let's not forget the women. They too have their own tours. And in the United States the US LPGA Tour offers prize money that, in some tournaments, outstrips that offered in some men's events. Such is the popularity of the ladies game in America.

The LPGA (formerly the Women's Professional Golf Association, WPGA) was formed in 1944 but it struggled in its first couple of years. It was only after assistance from the Wilson sports goods company, and Fred Corcoran in particular, that the organization was marketed in the right way and the fortunes of the Association took an upward turn.

By 1952 the number of tournaments was up to 21 (from seven two years earlier), and "Babe" Zaharias, Betsy Rawls, and Louise Suggs became household names. The arrival of Mickey Wright attracted a great deal of media attention in the 1960s and the women's game in America again boomed. And in 1963 the Tour benefited from the arrival of the television cameras.

However, the Tour expanded too quickly and it struggled to keep up with its expansion. In 1973 it had to be rescued from the verge of bankruptcy. The first commissioner, Ray Volpe, was appointed in 1975 and he set about seeking out corporate sponsors. He succeeded and, in his seven years as commissioner, prize money soared from $1.5 to $6.4 million. Television coverage increased, as did the number of touring professionals, and the ladies game in America went into the 1980s looking and feeling healthy.

Total purses from the 40-event schedule are in excess of $20 million and the top money winner banks a cheque approaching the $1 million mark. Pat Bradley, the highest-earning lady player, has amassed career winnings of $4,109,165.

The WPG European Tour however, does not enjoy the financial benefits of its American counterpart. It does not have the same sponsorship or television involvement as the US Tour, and consequently prize money and popularity are considerably lower. Sadly, in 1992 the tour programme had to be cut from 13 to 11 events because of sponsors' withdrawals. This compares to the 34 events on the US Women's tour in 1992.

THE BRITISH OPEN

THE WORLD'S FIRST Major, the British Open, was inaugurated in 1860 and was organized by the Prestwick club who sought to find a successor to Allan Robertson, the "champion of golf", who died in 1859. The only way to do that was by organizing an individual tournament, which was little heard of in those days. Most matches were foursomes or individual money matches.

But, in 1858 the Prestwick club had successfully organized an individual tournament for amateur players and, following the suggestion of Major J O Fairlie, a similar tournament for professionals was arranged. And on Wednesday 17 October 1860 eight of Britain's leading professionals played three rounds of Prestwick's 12-hole links.

The winner was Willie Park senior of the Musselburgh club. He was two strokes clear of local Prestwick man Tom Morris senior, who was to become one of the Open's great champions. Morris won the Open four times and was succeeded by his son, Young Tom, who also won the title on four occasions. But his untimely death at the age of 24 not only prevented him from adding to that total, but it robbed the game of one of its finest ever players.

The Open did not become open in the true sense of the word until

Top The Red Moroccan leather championship belt that became the permanent property of Young Tom Morris after his third British Open win in 1870

Above Young Tom proudly wearing the belt.

1861 when, again, organization was left to the Prestwick club. Old Tom Morris captured the title and he, like all early winners, was presented with a Moroccan leather belt donated by the Earl of Eglinton.

The rules stipulated that the winner of the Belt three years in succession could keep the trophy, and so after Young Tom Morris won for the third time in 1870 he

THE FIRST OPEN IN 1860

On Wednesday 17 October 1860, eight of Britain's top professionals met to play three rounds of Prestwick's 12-hole course.

Played in unsettled weather and in very windy conditions, Old Tom Morris of the host club was the first to tee off. Morris and Willie Park were the two favourites and after the first round Park led by three strokes, with a 55 to Morris's 58. The two men shot 59s in the second round as the Musselburgh man maintained his three-stroke advantage.

Morris was dogged by bad luck all day and he could only make up one stroke on the leader in the final round, as Willie Park became the first Open champion with a score of 174.

Two days later Morris beat Park by 7 & 6 in a £20 challenge match over the same 36 holes and thus regained some of his pride, and cash.

Scores
174 Willie Park, snr (Musselburgh)
176 Tom Morris, snr (Prestwick)
180 Andrew Strath (St Andrews)
191 Robert Andrew (Perth)
192 George Brown (Blackheath)
195 Charlie Hunter (Prestwick St Nicholas)
196 Alex Smith (Bruntsfield)
232 William Steel (Bruntsfield)

Below Nick Faldo after winning his second Open in 1990.

Above The Great Triumvirate of J H Taylor, James Braid and Harry Vardon. Between them they won the British Open 16 times.

THE OPEN'S GREATEST CHAMPIONS

Wins	Player	Nationality	Years
6	Harry Vardon	GB	1896, 1898-99, 1903, 1911, 1914
5	James Braid	GB	1901, 1905-06, 1908, 1910
5	John H Taylor	GB	1894-95, 1900, 1909, 1913
5	Peter Thomson	Aus	1954-56, 1958, 1965
5	Tom Watson	USA	1975, 1977, 1980, 1982-83
4	Tom Morris, snr	GB	1861-62, 1864, 1867
4	Tom Morris, jnr	GB	1868-70, 1872
4	Willie Park, snr	GB	1860, 1863, 1866, 1875
4	Walter Hagen	USA	1922, 1924, 1928-29
4	Bobby Locke	SAf	1949-50, 1952, 1957

was allowed to keep it. The following year, without a trophy to offer, there was no championship until revived in 1872 when Young Tom lifted the new silver claret jug which, today, remains one of the most sought-after trophies in world golf.

Having organized the first eleven competitions, the Prestwick club was finding it increasingly difficult to organize the event as the number of competitors grew and its popularity attracted more spectators. Consequently, the Royal and Ancient at St Andrews and the Honourable Company of Edinburgh Golfers, at Mussel-burgh, shared the organization and took it in turn to play hosts.

All Open courses are links and in 1894 the competition moved out of Scotland for the first time when Sandwich, in Kent, southern England, played host.

The first Open in England heralded the start of a domination of the championship by three men: John H Taylor, James Braid, and Harry Vardon. Known as The Great Triumvirate they captured 16 of the next 21 Opens.

It was after World War I that the switch in dominance moved from home-grown players to the Americans, and the breakthrough came in 1921 when Jock Hutchison became the first man to take the trophy across the Atlantic.

The 1920s and 30s was a golden age for American golfers with Jim Barnes, Walter Hagen, Tommy Armour, Gene Sarazen and Denny Shute all capturing the title. And there was also the world's greatest ever amateur golfer, Robert Tyre "Bobby" Jones, who won the Open three times between 1926 and 1930. The latter year was a remarkable

one for the Georgia lawyer because he captured the Opens, as well as the amateur titles, of both Britain and America.

The early post-war years belonged to Commonwealth golfers Bobby Locke of South Africa and Australia's Peter Thomson, who won nine titles between them, with Thomson's five wins being the best haul since the days of Taylor, Braid and Vardon.

Sadly, American interest declined in the 1950s but Arnold Palmer set about maintaining the British Open's stature as the world's leading golf tournament and his arrival on the scene aroused great interest in the game in general. He also ensured that many top Americans made the trip across the Atlantic every summer. Palmer was rewarded with successive titles in 1961 and 1962.

Palmer's arrival on British shores was also to signal the birth of the next golfing triumvirate as he, Gary Player of South Africa, and Palmer's compatriot Jack Nicklaus became great favourites with the British fans. They won eight British Open titles between them; Player doing so in three different decades, the 1950s, 60s, and 70s.

Britain had her rare moment of glory when Tony Jacklin ended an 18-year drought in 1969 by taking

the title from the left-handed New Zealander Bob Charles at Lytham. But that was a rare moment of success as the Americans continued to dominate, with Tom Watson winning a modern-day record five titles. But the 1980s saw a switch away from the Americans as first Sandy Lyle, and then Nick Faldo three times, put the trophy back in British hands. Spain has also enjoyed her moment of glory thanks to Severiano Ballesteros's three titles and, in recent years, Greg Norman and Ian Baker-Finch have brought Australia back to the forefront of world golf.

THE OPEN COURSES

Course (Country)	Times used	First used	Last used
Prestwick (Scotland)	24	1860	1925
St Andrews (Scotland)	24	1873	1990
Muirfield (Scotland)	14	1892	1992
Sandwich (England)	11	1894	1985
Hoylake (England)	10	1897	1967
Lytham (England)	8	1926	1988
Birkdale (England)	7	1954	1991
Musselburgh (Scotland)	6	1874	1889
Troon (Scotland)	6	1923	1989
Carnoustie (Scotland)	5	1931	1975
Deal (England)	2	1909	1920
Turnberry (Scotland)	2	1977	1986
Prince's (England)	1	1932	1932
Portrush (N. Ireland)	1	1951	1951

OPEN RECORDS

Lowest 18-hole total:	63	Mark Hayes, Turnberry 1977
	63	Isao Aoki, Muirfield 1980
	63	Greg Norman, Turnberry 1986
	63	Paul Broadhurst, St Andrews 1990
	63	Jodie Mudd, Birkdale 1991
Lowest 72-hole total:	268	Tom Watson, Turnberry 1977
Oldest winner:	46 yrs 3 mths	Tom Morris, snr, 1867
Youngest winner:	17 yrs 8 mths	Tom Morris, jnr, 1868

TURNBERRY 1977 – RECORDS GALORE

Turnberry, situated on the West Coast of Scotland and with the beautiful scenic backdrop of Ailsa Craig, the Mull of Kintyre and the Isle of Arran, was a long time in being added to the list of British Open courses. But when it did arrive in 1977 it was the scene of record scoring, the likes of which had not been seen before.

The Open record for 72 holes previously stood at 276, courtesy of Messrs Palmer and Weiskopf. But the first two men home at Turnberry covered the 6,875 yard Ailsa course in 268 and 269 respectively, with the champion Tom Watson lowering the Championship record by eight strokes.

The opening round belonged to John Schroeder, son of the 1949 Wimbledon singles champion Ted Schroeder, who shot an opening 66 to take the lead. But he took a back seat on day two as America's Mark Hayes became the first man to shoot a 63 in the Open and thus lower the old record by two strokes, which had stood since Henry Cotton shot the first 65 way back in 1934.

While Hayes was setting his record-breaking round the big guns of Tom Watson and Jack Nicklaus (pictured above) were making their way up the leader board. They both had third round 65s, after each had opening rounds of

68 and 70, and they set up a wonderful final day. The large crowds were not disappointed as both men played memorable golf, with Watson's final round 65 edging out Nicklaus by one stroke.

In addition to Hayes' record 63, and Watson's four round record 268, Watson's 130 for the last two rounds was a record, his 200 for the last 54 holes was also a record and he and Nicklaus shared the record low score for the first 54 holes. The crowd of 92,000 was also a record for a Scottish course. Turnberry's first Open was certainly a record-breaking one!

UNITED STATES OPEN

THE FORERUNNER OF the US Open took place in 1894 when Willie Dunn won a matchplay event. However, the first championship carrying the US Open name was held at Newport, Rhode Island on 4 October 1895. It was scheduled for the previous month but that clashed with the America's Cup which was taking place at Rhode Island at the same time.

The first Open was over four rounds of Newport's 9-hole course and the winner from a field of ten professionals and one amateur was English-born Horace Rawlins, who took the first prize of $150 with a 36-hole total of 173.

The first 16 Opens were all won by British-born golfers, and when Harry Vardon made the journey across the Atlantic to take the title in 1900 he did a great deal to help popularize the game in America.

In 1911, a home-bred player captured the title for the first time when Johnny McDermott won a three-way play-off.

McDermott retained his title in 1912 and the following year, victory by an unknown amateur

changed the course of golfing history in the United States.

Twenty-year-old Francis Ouimet lived across the road from the Brookline Country Club, venue for the 1913 Open. He entered the competition without realistically expecting to have any impact on the big names of the world of professional golf, including Britain's top golfers Vardon and Ted Ray. But what a

memorable occasion it was as Ouimet shared the lead after 72 holes and then went on to beat the Britons by five and six strokes respectively in the play-off. The British domination of world golf was over and that is how it stayed for 70 years, give or take the odd hiccup.

Ted Ray took the title back to Britain in 1920, but that was it until Tony Jacklin's success in 1970. Since then no Briton has captured the US title and, since Jacklin's victory, only Australia's David Graham in 1981 has broken the American stranglehold.

Bobby Jones, Ben Hogan and Jack Nicklaus, three of the biggest names in world golf, have all won the Open four times. Hogan's 1950 success, less than two years after a near-fatal car accident, was one of the most emotional in the tournament's long history.

Above Bobby Jones (right) after completing the game's most remarkable Grand Slam in 1930.

Left Britain's Ted Ray, the 1920 US Open winner.

Above 'She's all mine'. Curtis Strange after capturing his first US Open title in 1988. He won the title again in 1989 to become the first back-to-back winner since Ben Hogan in 1951.

Left Sam Snead in action during the first post-war British Open, at St Andrews in 1946. He went on to win the title from Bobby Locke and Johnny Bulla.

SAM SNEAD'S CATALOGUE OF NEAR MISSES

In terms of wins, Sam Snead is the most successful golfer in US history, with 81 Tour wins during his long career. But, remarkably, the man who has won seven Majors has never won the US Open. Even more surprising, he finished second in his very first Open in 1937, and many thought that after such a start the title would be a formality one day. But it was not to be.

These are Sam Snead's near misses in the US Open.

1937 Oakland Hills, Michigan

281	Ralph Guldahl	71	69	72	69
283	Sam Snead	69	73	70	71
285	Bobby Cruickshank	73	73	67	72

1947 St Louis, Missouri

282	Lew Worsham	70	70	71	71
282	Sam Snead	72	70	70	70
Worsham won play-off 69-70					
285	Bobby Locke	68	74	70	73
285	Porky Oliver	73	70	71	71

1949 Medinah, Illinois

286	Cary Middlecoff	75	67	69	75
287	Sam Snead	73	73	71	70
287	Clayton Heafner	72	71	71	73

1953 Oakmont, Pennsylvania

283	Ben Hogan	67	72	73	71
289	Sam Snead	72	69	72	76
292	Lloyd Mangrum	73	70	74	75

The nearest Snead came was in 1947. He holed an 18-foot putt on the 72nd hole to force the play-off with Worsham. But on the same hole in the play-off he missed from less than a yard, and lost by one stroke.

OPEN RECORDS

Lowest 18-hole total:	63 Johnny Miller, Oakmont 1973	
	63 Tom Weiskopf, Baltusrol 1980	
	63 Jack Nicklaus, Baltusrol 1980	
Lowest 72-hole total:	272 Jack Nicklaus, Baltusrol 1980	
Oldest winner:	45 yrs Hale Irwin, 1990	
Youngest winner:	19 yrs 10 mths Johnny McDermott, 1911	

US MASTERS

THE MASTERS IS the youngest of the four Majors. It is the only one that is by invitation only, and the only one played on the same course each year - the wonderful setting of the Augusta National course in Georgia.

The Masters and the Augusta National were the brainchild of Bobby Jones. The course was designed and constructed by Alister Mackenzie on a site that was formerly a nursery and the reminder of its former days is evident in the abundance of beautiful shrubs, bushes, trees and flowers that line the course. Each hole is named after the plant life adjacent to it.

The first Masters, back in 1934, attracted very little interest and in an effort to arouse media attention Bobby Jones came out of retirement. The first winner was Horton Smith, who snatched a last gasp win from Craig Wood thanks to finishing birdie-par.

Wood was again runner-up in the second year after losing a play-off to Gene Sarazen, whose double eagle at the par-5 15th is one of the most talked-about shots.

To win the coveted green jacket that is presented to the Masters champion each year requires the best of concentration because the course, with its narrow fairways and abundance of bunkers and water, poses the sternest of tests. And one man who has passed that test not once but a staggering six

Above The US Masters Trophy.

Below left Severiano Ballesteros putting to win in 1980.

Below right Nick Price shooting a Masters record 63 in 1986.

MASTERS RECORDS

Lowest 18-hole total:	63	Nick Price, 1986
Lowest 72-hole total:	271	Jack Nicklaus, 1965
	271	Ray Floyd, 1976
Oldest winner:	46 yrs 2 mths	Jack Nicklaus, 1986
Youngest winner:	23 yrs 0 mths	Seve Ballesteros, 1980

times is Jack Nicklaus. His sixth victory came at the age of 46 in 1986.

Gary Player was the first non-American winner of the Masters in 1961 and he won it on two more occasions, but no other non-American won until Severiano Ballesteros took the title in 1980. This heralded the start of a European domination which shook the American golfing world. Ballesteros won again in 1983. Germany's Bernhard Langer won in 1985 and between 1988 and 1991 British players won four consecutive titles thanks to Sandy Lyle, Ian Woosnam and Nick Faldo, who emulated the great Jack Nicklaus by winning back-to-back titles. Fred Couples, however, arrested the situation in 1992 by recapturing the title for the home players.

JACK NICKLAUS - THE MASTER OF AUGUSTA

Jack Nicklaus has won the Masters a record six times. These are details of his wins:

1963

286	Jack Nicklaus	74	66	74	72
287	Tony Lema	74	69	74	70

1965

271	Jack Nicklaus	67	71	64	69
280	Arnold Palmer	70	68	72	70
280	Gary Player	65	73	69	73

1966

288	Jack Nicklaus	68	76	72	72
288	Tommy Jacobs	75	71	70	72
288	Gay Brewer	74	72	72	70

Nicklaus won play-off 70-72-78

1972

286	Jack Nicklaus	68	71	73	74
289	Tom Weiskopf	74	71	70	74
289	Bruce Crampton	72	75	69	73
289	Bobby Mitchell	73	72	71	73

1975

276	Jack Nicklaus	68	67	73	68
277	Johnny Miller	75	71	65	66
277	Tom Weiskopf	69	72	66	70

1986

279	Jack Nicklaus	74	71	69	65
280	Greg Norman	70	72	68	70
280	Tom Kite	70	74	68	68

In addition to his six wins Nicklaus finished second or joint second four times, in 1964, 1971, 1977, 1981. Right, Langer helps Nicklaus don the coveted green jacket in 1986.

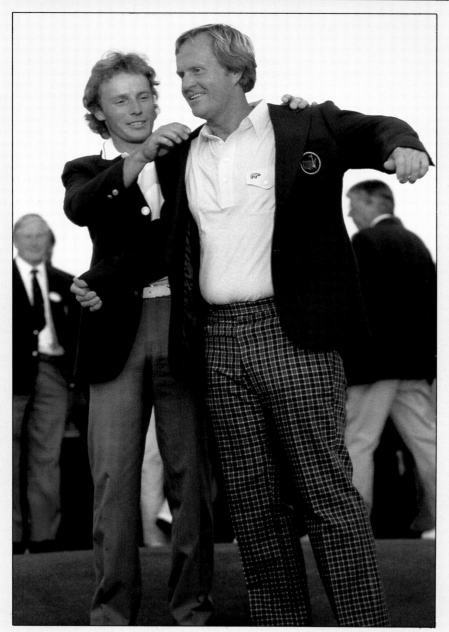

THE US PGA CHAMPIONSHIP

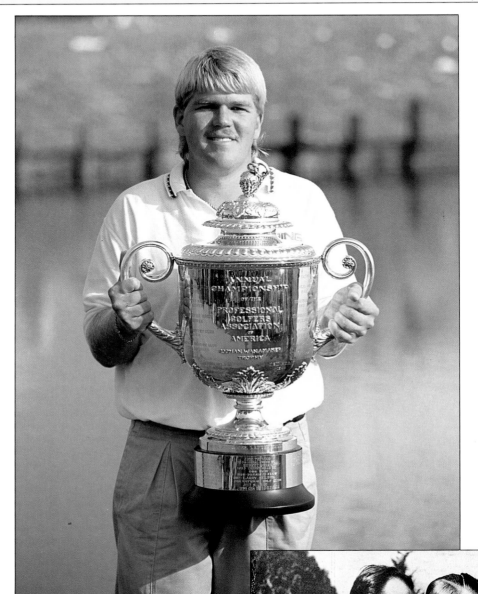

THE LEAST PRESTIGIOUS of the four Majors, the US PGA Championship, is nevertheless a much sought-after trophy by American golfers. Qualification for the PGA Championship is based on performances on the US Tour which, effectively, makes it a very Americanized event. To date only Gary Player of South Africa, Nick Price of Zimbabwe and the Australian pair of David Graham and Wayne Grady have been non-American winners.

The first PGA Championship was in 1916, the year of the formation of the US Professional Golfers Association. One of the biggest attractions of winning the Championship, apart from the large cheque that accompanies success, is future exemption from pre-qualifying for all US Tour events. That in itself is worth a great deal.

From its inauguration until 1958, the Championship was a matchplay event, and in the 1920s Walter Hagen proved himself to be one of the finest exponents of this form of golf by taking the title five times in seven years between 1921 and 1927. Between 1924 and

Above John Daly, the big-hitting surprise winner of the US PGA Championship in 1991.

Right Paul Runyan (centre), winner of the 1938 PGA Championship receives his trophy after beating Sam Snead (looking on left) in the final at Shawnee Country Club.

WALTER HAGEN – THE MATCHPLAY EXPERT

Between 1921 and 1927 Walter Hagen competed in six of the seven US PGA Championships that were held. He won five of the six in which he competed and was beaten finalist in the other. This is his amazing record.

1921 Inwood, New York
Final: Walter Hagen beat Jim Barnes 3 & 2

1922 Oakmont, Pennsylvania
Did not compete

1923 Pelham, New York
Final: Gene Sarazen beat Walter Hagen at 38th hole

1924 French Lick, Indiana
Final: Walter Hagen beat Jim Barnes 2 up

1925 Olympia Fields, Illinois
Final: Walter Hagen beat Bill Melhorn 6 & 5

1926 Salisbury, New York
Final: Walter Hagen beat Leo Diegel 5 & 3

1927 Cedar Crest, Texas
Final: Walter Hagen beat Joe Turnesa 1 up

His run of 22 consecutive wins came to an end in the quarter-final in 1928 when beaten by Leo Diegel.

1928, when he lost in the quarter-finals, Hagen went 22 consecutive matches without defeat against the cream of the US professionals. When he lost, the PGA asked him for the trophy back and he replied by saying that he had left it in the back of a taxi a couple of years earlier! The trophy was eventually recovered.

In 1980 Jack Nicklaus equalled Hagen's record of five wins. But it is the one Major that Arnold Palmer never captured.

For drama, the final of the 1930 Championship between Gene Sarazen and Tommy Armour takes some beating. The two stalwarts engaged in a wonderfully close battle for 35 holes. At the last, Armour holed a putt from 14 feet (4.2 m). Sarazen then had a similar putt but missed by inches, and with it went the title.

Now a strokeplay event, like the other Majors, the PGA has a regular August date each year and is the last of the season's four Majors. But at one time it used to either clash with or be played within a week of the British Open, and for this reason Ben Hogan was deprived of the chance of winning all four Majors in 1953.

PGA RECORDS

Lowest 18-hole total:	63	Bruce Crampton, Firestone 1975
	63	Ray Floyd, Southern Hills 1982
	63	Gary Player, Shoal Creek 1984
Lowest 72-hole total:	271	Bobby Nichols, Columbus 1964
Oldest winner:	48 yrs 5 mths	Julius Boros, 1968
Youngest winner:	20 yrs 6 mths	Gene Sarazen, 1922

RYDER CUP

THE WORLD'S LEADING professional team tournament, the Ryder Cup, has aroused a great deal of interest both sides of the Atlantic in recent years, particularly as the American domination which lasted over 20 years eventually came to an end in the 1980s. And for the first time since the Cup's early days, it is no longer a one-sided affair.

The forerunner of the Ryder Cup was a match between professional teams from Britain and America at Wentworth in 1926. The British team won 13½ to 1½. This match led to English seed merchant Samuel Ryder suggesting a biennial tournament between the two nations, held alternately on each side of the Atlantic. And so was born the Ryder Cup, with the first official match taking place at Worcester, Massachusetts on 3-4 June 1927.

Ryder's interest in golf started when he suffered ill-health while living in Hertfordshire, England. Upon the suggestion of a local church minister, the Reverend Frank Wheeler, he joined the St Albans Verulam Golf Club and

Left The most famous international golfing team trophy, the Ryder Cup.

Below Walter Hagen holds the trophy after the USA won the first Ryder Cup in 1927.

suddenly golf became the new love of his life.

He befriended some of the day's great golfers, Braid, Taylor, Vardon, and local professional Abe Mitchell. The statue on top of the Ryder Cup trophy is modelled on Mitchell.

The Americans won the first Ryder Cup, Britain won the next on home soil, and so it went for the first four times with the home team winning on each occasion. But that all changed in 1937 when the Americans won on British soil for the first time, winning 8-4 at Southport & Ainsdale. Britain did not gain their next win until 1957 when skippered by Dai Rees. But that was it; the Americans dominated for the next two decades.

The competition became too one-sided, with the British team suffering some heavy defeats. In

Above Opposing captains J H Taylor (left) and Walter Hagen shake hands before the 1933 Ryder Cup at Southport & Ainsdale. The man who started it all, Samuel Ryder, is in the middle.

Below A joyous Dai Rees after Britain won the Ryder Cup in 1957.

an attempt to arrest the decline of the competition it was agreed that from 1979 European golfers could compete. And America's opponents became Europe instead of Great Britain and Ireland.

The change did little initially as the Americans continued to take charge but in 1983, under new captain Tony Jacklin, the Europeans came within a point of their first win since 1957. Two years later at The Belfry, Jacklin enjoyed one of his finest moments when he led the side to victory, thus ending a 28-year drought. But more was to come as Jacklin and his men retained the trophy two years later and thus became the first team to defeat the Americans on home soil.

By now interest in the Ryder Cup was greater than ever, and back at The Belfry in 1989 an intense battle resulted in only the second tied Cup but, as defending champions, the Europeans managed to keep their hands on their trophy. In 1991, however, the Americans wrested it back. But long gone are the days when they could be assured of holding on to it, and the hype surrounding the event every two years makes the Ryder Cup one of the greatest occasions on the golfing calendar.

Below A delighted European team after winning the 1989 Ryder Cup . . . and so they should be, they retained the trophy after drawing 14 all at The Belfry.

Bottom right Tony Jacklin savours one of the greatest moments in his career after guiding the European team to their first Ryder Cup success in 1985, and thus inflicted the first defeat on the Americans for 28 years.

THE RYDER CUP 1985 EUROPEAN TEAM

After a 28-year monopoly, the Americans lost their grip on the Ryder Cup in 1985 when Tony Jacklin's men won by five points at The Belfry. This is how victory was achieved. *European names first*

DAY ONE
Foursomes
Severiano Ballesteros & Manuel Pinero beat Curtis Strange & Mark O'Meara 2 & 1
Bernhard Langer & Nick Faldo lost to Calvin Peete & Tom Kite 3 & 2
Sandy Lyle & Ken Brown lost to Lanny Wadkins & Ray Floyd 4 & 3
Howard Clark & Sam Torrance lost to Craig Stadler & Hal Sutton 3 & 2
Score: Europe 1 UNITED STATES 3

Fourballs
Paul Way & Ian Woosnam beat Fuzzy Zoeller & Hubert Green 1 hole
Severiano Ballesteros & Manuel Pinero beat Andy North & Peter Jacobsen 2 & 1
Bernhard Langer & José Maria Canizares halved with Craig Stadler & Hal Sutton
Sam Torrance & Howard Clark lost to Ray Floyd & Lanny Wadkins 1 hole
Score: Europe 3½ UNITED STATES 4½

DAY TWO
Fourballs
Sam Torrance & Howard Clark beat Tom Kite & Andy North 2 & 1
Paul Way & Ian Woosnam beat Hubert Green & Fuzzy Zoeller 4 & 3
Severiano Ballesteros & Manuel Pinero lost to Mark O'Meara & Lanny Wadkins 3 & 2
Bernhard Langer & Sandy Lyle halved with Curtis Strange & Craig Stadler
Score: Europe 6 United States 6

Foursomes
José Maria Canizares & José Rivero beat Tom Kite & Calvin Peete 7 & 5
Severiano Ballesteros & Manuel Pinero beat Craig Stadler & Hal Sutton 5 & 4
Paul Way & Ian Woosnam lost to Curtis Strange & Peter Jacobsen 4 & 2
Bernhard Langer & Ken Brown beat Ray Floyd & Lanny Wadkins 3 & 2
Score: EUROPE 9 United States 7

DAY THREE
Singles
Manuel Pinero beat Lanny Wadkins 3 & 1
Ian Woosnam lost to Craig Stadler 2 & 1
Paul Way beat Ray Floyd 2 holes
Severiano Ballesteros halved with Tom Kite
Sandy Lyle beat Peter Jacobsen 3 & 2
Bernhard Langer beat Hal Sutton 5 & 4
Sam Torrance beat Andy North 1 hole
Howard Clark beat Mark O'Meara 1 hole
José Rivero lost to Calvin Peete 1 hole
Nick Faldo lost to Hubert Green 3 & 1
José Maria Canizares beat Fuzzy Zoeller 2 holes
Ken Brown lost to Curtis Strange 4 & 2
FINAL SCORE: EUROPE 16½ United States 11½

WORLD MATCHPLAY CHAMPIONSHIP

capturing the title five times between 1965 and 1973. His record of five wins was equalled by Spain's Severiano Ballesteros in 1991.

One of the most memorable moments of the World Matchplay was in 1979 when Japan's Isao Aoki, the eventual beaten finalist, holed-in-one at the second. His feat saw him win a £55,000

Left Arnold Palmer, winner of the first World Matchplay title in 1964.

Below The 'Master of Wentworth' Gary Player after beating Graham Marsh to win his fifth World Matchplay title in 1973.

MATCHPLAY GOLF IS very popular at club level, but amongst professionals it is played in a small handful of major competitions. The Ryder Cup, of course, is all played to matchplay rules, but the world's leading individual tournament is unquestionably the World Matchplay Championship played at Wentworth each October. It is an invitational event with the crop of the world's golfers taking part.

First held in 1964 it was originally sponsored by Piccadilly, who remained with the event until 1977 when succeeded by Colgate. Between 1979 and 1990 the sponsors were Suntory and since 1991 have been the Japanese car manufacturer Toyota.

Arnold Palmer was the inaugural champion, beating Britain's Neil Coles in the first final. Britain had to wait until 1987 for her first champion when Ian Woosnam beat fellow Briton Sandy Lyle in the final.

Gary Player was the master of matchplay in the 1960s and 70s,

furnished flat overlooking the
Wentworth course.

HOW IT IS PLAYED

Twelve invited players take part
each year with four receiving "top
seed status". Those four do not
take part in the first round and
"receive a bye" into the second.
The other eight fight it out on a
straight knockout basis. The four
winners then join the four seeds in
the second round and it continues
as a knockout tournament.
Matches are over 36 holes. If a
match is not resolved after two
complete rounds then it is decided
on a "sudden death" basis.

Above Ian Woosnam looks delighted
with his 1987 Suntory Trophy.

Right Seve Ballesteros at the 1991
World Matchplay.

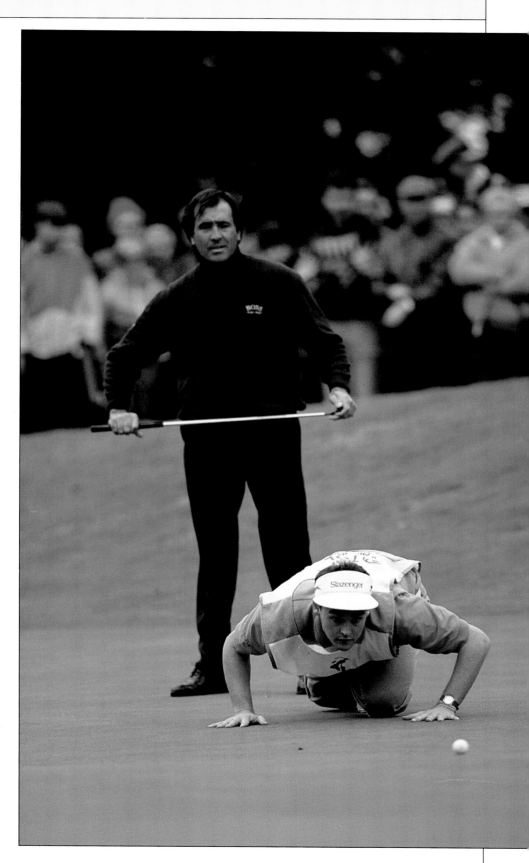

WOMEN'S MAJORS

THERE ARE FOUR women's Majors, and all four are played in the United States.

The most prestigious is the US WOMEN'S OPEN, inaugurated in 1946, four years before the formation of the US LPGA. The first winner was Patty Berg who beat Betty Jameson 5 and 4 in the final on the only occasion it was played under matchplay rules. Mickey Wright and Betsy Rawls have each won the Open a record four times.

The LPGA CHAMPIONSHIP was first held in 1955 and, like the Open, was a matchplay event in its first year and was won by Beverly Hanson. Mickey Wright, with four wins, has been the most successful golfer in LPGA championships.

The DU MAURIER CLASSIC started life as the La Canadienne in 1973 and was known as the Peter Jackson Classic between 1974 and 1982. And it was during that time that it was granted Major status, in 1979, and won by Amy Alcott. Pat Bradley, in 1980, 1985 and 1986, has won it a record three times.

The newest of the four Majors is the NABISCO DINAH SHORE which was designated a Major in 1983 after changing its name from the Colgate-Dinah Shore, which had been inaugurated in 1972. The first winner of the event as a Major was, again, Amy Alcott who won it for a record third time in 1991.

One of the most successful lady golfers in the 1980s was America's Amy Alcott. She won three Majors during the decade including the 1980 US Women's Open.

Right America's Nancy Lopez has been successful both sides of the Atlantic. She is seen here after capturing the 1979 LPGA title at Sunningdale, England.

Below Pat Bradley, winner of the du Maurier Classic a record three times between 1980 and 1986, including back-to-back wins in '85 and '86.

DID YOU KNOW?

The highest score ever recorded for a single hole is 166, achieved over 80 years ago by a woman player from Pennsylvania, USA. Many of the strokes were made from a rowing boat while her ball floated a mile and a half down a river.

THE WORLD'S OUTSTANDING GOLF COURSES

GOLF IS BLESSED with so many wonderful golf courses that it is difficult to know where in the world to begin. So we'll take the most uncontroversial way out and present them in alphabetical order by country as follows:

AUSTRALIA
CANADA
EIRE
ENGLAND
FRANCE
NORTHERN IRELAND
PORTUGAL
SCOTLAND
SPAIN
SWITZERLAND
UNITED STATES

Each entry includes a map of the course showing bunkers, water hazards, fairways, clubhouse and numbered tees as well as pictures of the course and a score card.

ROYAL MELBOURNE

ONE OF THE finest golf courses outside Britain or America is the Royal Melbourne Club, which has continual membership dating from July 1891.

The official outfit for all members in those early days was a scarlet coat with gold buttons, knickerbockers, and Tam O'Shanter, thus confirming the Scottish connection.

The course moved to the Sandringham district of Melbourne in 1901 and a new course was laid out. Its deep bunkers turned it into one of the great championship courses in the world.

While retaining some characteristics of Scottish links, it also has some of the beauty of the Augusta National course. But that is hardly surprising because the man hired by Bobby Jones to design Augusta, Alister

Mackenzie, was also hired to design the new course at Melbourne in the 1920s. The second, East, course, was added in 1932 and the original course was named the West course.

Such is the design of the two that holes from both can be incorporated into one 18-hole course for major championships.

The greens at Melbourne are lifted every six years to ensure their trueness and, consequently, they are lightning fast. And for a true test of a golfer's ability and nerve the 6th and 14th holes provide a daunting task. Both are doglegs; the first requires the decision to play short of, or attempt to negotiate, some awkwardly placed bunkers. The latter is a 90-degree dogleg, but trees lining the right-hand side of the fairway make it difficult to assess the correct line.

THE ROYAL COURSES HOW THEY BECAME "ROYAL"

A golf club cannot adopt the word "Royal" in its title unless this right has been bestowed upon it by the sovereign or a member of the Royal house. This is normally granted when a club receives Royal patronage.

The Perth Golfing Society was, in 1833, the first club to be granted Royal designation. There are now 36 Royal golf courses in the British Isles.

Right The fabulous setting of the 5th on Royal Melbourne's West Course.

SCORECARD

Hole	Metres	Par	Hole	Metres	Par
1	392	4	10	425	4
2	443	5	11	401	4
3	304	4	12	396	4
4	402	4	13	324	4
5	161	3	14	433	4
6	391	4	15	350	4
7	135	3	16	184	3
8	279	4	17	510	5
9	416	4	18	395	4
Out	2,923	35	In	3,418	36
TOTALS				6,341	71

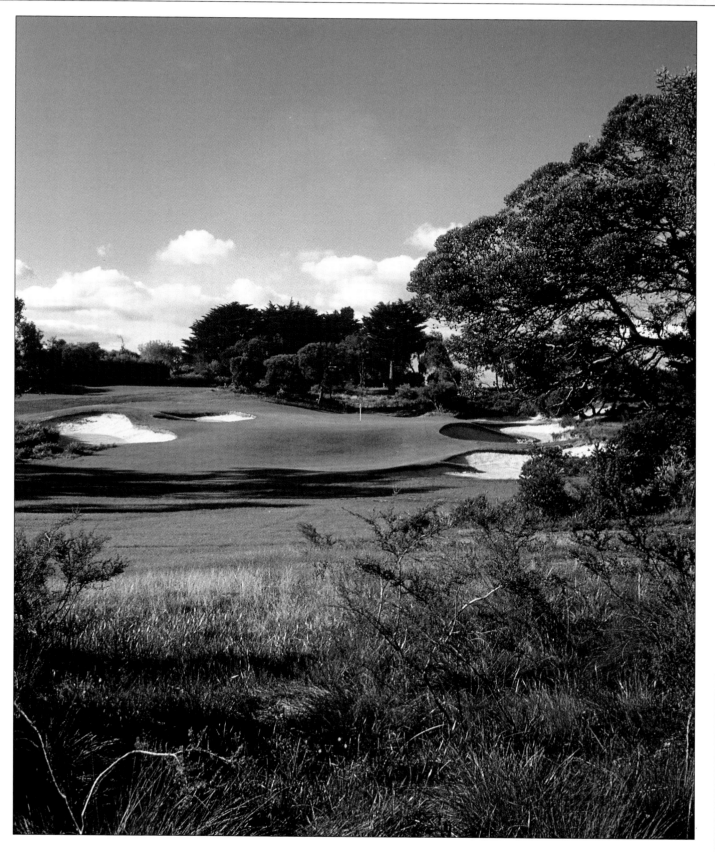

GLEN ABBEY

SITUATED AT OAKVILLE, Ontario, Glen Abbey became the home of the Canadian Open in 1977 and, except for 1980, has been its permanent home ever since.

The course was one of the first to be purpose-built to meet the demands of modern-day golf in the 1970s, when Jack Nicklaus was asked to design a course taking in the Sixteen Mile Creek close to Lake Ontario.

It is a spectacular course, and Nicklaus took full advantage of the natural beauty of the area. Such is the appeal of the place that the Golf House, formerly a Jesuit retreat, is the home of the Royal Canadian Golf Association.

Nicklaus designed the course with the spectator in mind, and banked areas behind the greens are a feature. Also, many of the greens and tees are within close proximity of the clubhouse.

Huge crowds attend the Canadian Open each year, regarded by many as the fifth major, and the large areas between the fairways help with the problem of crowd congestion caused at many golf courses.

Nicklaus was not left to start from scratch because there had been a course on the site since the

SCORECARD					
Hole	Yards	Par	Hole	Yards	Par
1	369	4	10	435	5
2	380	4	11	426	4
3	123	3	12	152	3
4	345	4	13	481	5
5	452	5	14	330	4
6	395	4	15	115	3
7	135	3	16	452	5
8	391	4	17	365	4
9	383	4	18	461	5
Out	2,973	35	In	3,217	38
TOTALS				6,190	73

early 1960s when the Jesuits sold the land. But Nicklaus's task was a major rebuilding one.

The natural terrain of the ravine has been fully utilized and the 11th to 15th holes, known as the Valley, are the toughest on the course. The short 15th, although only 140 yards from the back tee, is extremely tough. The green slopes from back to front but bunkers at back and front make correct club selection crucial.

The course opened in June 1976 when designer Nicklaus played an exhibition match with the reigning Canadian Open champion Tom Weiskopf.

Left Glen Abbey's 13th.

Below What a closing hole! The 18th at Glen Abbey. Even Lawrence of Arabia wouldn't have survived in that lot!

> **DID YOU KNOW?**
>
> *There have been some notable golf non-enthusiasts as the following quotes reveal: "An expensive way of playing marbles," G K Chesterton. "An ineffectual attempt to direct an uncontrollable sphere into an inaccessible hole with instruments ill-adapted to the purpose," Sir Winston Churchill. "A good walk spoiled," Mark Twain.*

THE NATIONAL

ALREADY THE NATIONAL is regarded as one of the top Canadian golf courses yet it was only constructed in 1973.

The course was designed by Tom Fazio, nephew of the former professional and course designer George Fazio, who offered plenty of advice to his nephew during the construction of the National.

The idea of a course at Woodbridge, Ontario, came from car parts manufacturer Gil Blechman, who was fed up with the way of life in suburban Toronto golf and country clubs. He decided it was time to build a "proper" golf club and he set about fulfilling that dream. His instructions to Fazio were simple: "Build me the best golf course in the world."

The site for the new course was Pine Valley, which was already laid out for golf, but it was nothing like the splendour of its New Jersey namesake. The Pine Valley course was not totally suitable, but when Fazio spotted some adjacent land he knew that Blechman's dream could be realized.

The additional land gave an extra five holes. They are regarded as the toughest in the whole of Canada, but Fazio also managed to incorporate some majestic scenery into them.

Although completed in 1973 the National Golf Club was not officially opened for play until 1975. The idea that Blechman had of building a golf course without the other distractions of the "country club atmosphere" are clearly visible at the National. Golf is what the National is for, nothing else.

Water hazards affect nine of the 18 holes, and the outward nine are long and tough, with the wind making them even more difficult

on certain days. Because of the natural terrain, the back nine holes are situated some 100 feet below the front nine and the natural hills make it possible for more than 50,000 spectators to fill the course at any one time.

One of the finest testaments to the National's design came shortly after it was opened, when all the players in a tournament for leading local amateurs were asked to name the best hole on the course. The result showed 14 different answers.

SCORECARD					
Hole	Yards	Par	Hole	Yards	Par
1	388	4	10	176	3
2	427	4	11	406	4
3	424	4	12	503	5
4	581	5	13	379	4
5	205	3	14	421	4
6	531	5	15	221	3
7	445	4	16	384	4
8	190	3	17	428	4
9	425	4	18	455	5
Out	3,616	36	In	3,373	36
TOTALS				6,989	72

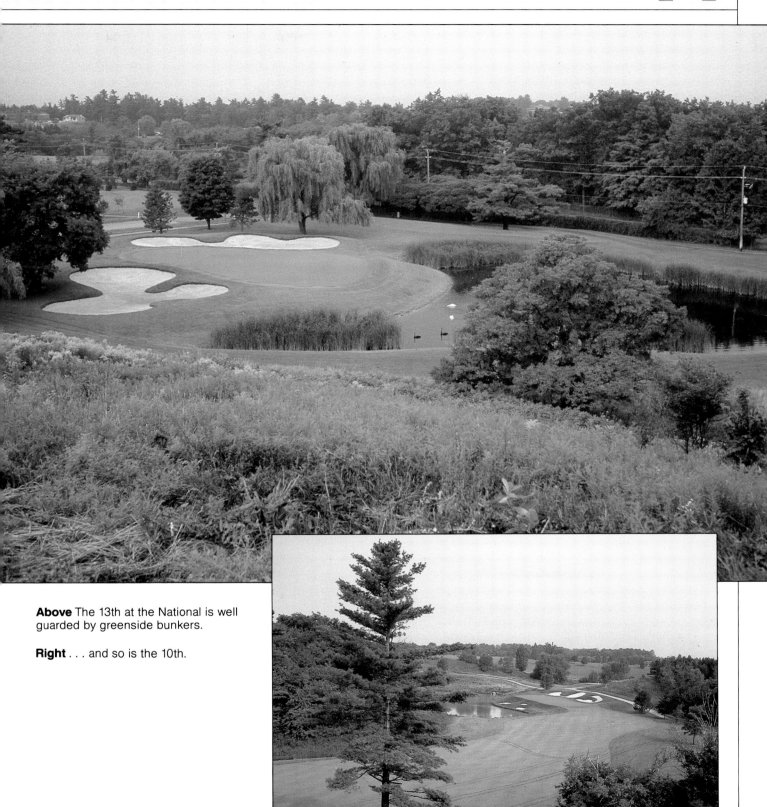

Above The 13th at the National is well
guarded by greenside bunkers.

Right . . . and so is the 10th.

BALLYBUNION

SET AMONGST SUCH beauty and splendour, the natural assets of the Kerry coastline have been fully utilized in designing and building the course. Its admirers have described Ballybunion as "the best golf course in the world". That is a very bold claim but there is no doubting its standing as one of the really great links courses.

Situated on the Atlantic coast of the Republic of Ireland in County Kerry, the course commands beautiful views out on to the ocean and is a very popular course with British and European golfers.

Many of the holes, particularly those alongside the edge of the ocean, are lined with huge sandhills which give the feeling of playing in a vast amphitheatre.

The club dates to 1893 but after five years it folded following financial difficulties. However, it was re-formed in 1906 by a retired Indian Army officer, Colonel Bartholomew, and a few friends. They brought in Lionel Hewson to lay out a new nine-hole course. It was not until 1927 that it became a full 18-hole course but by the 1930s it had become a championship course when Betty Lachford won the Irish Ladies title there.

A new clubhouse was built in

Set on the Atlantic coast of Southern Ireland, Ballybunion's Old Course is a testing links course.

1971 and the order of the holes was changed that same year, with play starting at what was the original 14th hole.

Uphill, downhill and sideway lies amongst the undulating terrain make Ballybunion a difficult course. But a look around also confirms it as one of the most beautiful.

SCORECARD					
Hole	Yards	Par	Hole	Yards	Par
1	392	4	10	359	4
2	445	4	11	449	4
3	220	3	12	192	3
4	498	5	13	484	5
5	508	5	14	131	3
6	364	4	15	216	3
7	423	4	16	490	5
8	153	3	17	385	4
9	454	4	18	379	4
Out	3,457	36	In	3,085	35
TOTALS				6,542	71

Ballybunion Old Course

PORTMARNOCK

ONE OF THE venues for the Irish Open, Portmarnock played host to the very first championship in 1927 when George Duncan won with a score of 312.

Situated in Co. Dublin, Portmarnock is not one of the most spectacular Irish golf courses, but certainly rates as one of the "greats". Bobby Locke, that outstanding South African golfer, once rated it amongst the best in Europe.

The site for the course was found by accident. Two men, named Ross and Pickeman, came across the expanse of land while out in a boat in 1893. Access to the land was solely by boat. However, the two intrepid explorers took a fancy to the land and by the end of the year they had formed a golf club.

Apart from playing host to the Irish Open, Portmarnock has staged the British Amateur Championship and in 1960 Arnold Palmer made his first appearance in Europe when he played in the winning United States World Cup team alongside Sam Snead.

For many years the Portmarnock professional was Harry Bradshaw.

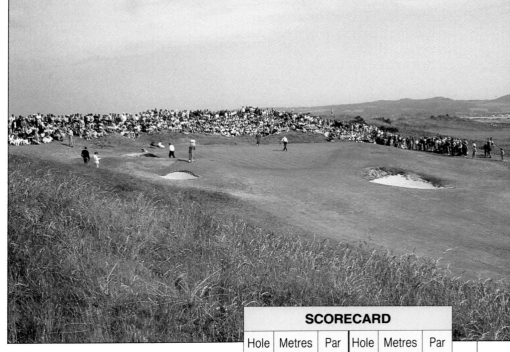

Although not a venue for the British Open, Portmarnock in Co. Dublin has staged many major championships including the British Amateur Championship and the World Cup.

SCORECARD

Hole	Metres	Par	Hole	Metres	Par
1	358	4	10	341	4
2	346	4	11	389	4
3	351	4	12	136	3
4	407	4	13	516	5
5	364	4	14	359	4
6	550	5	15	191	3
7	161	3	16	484	5
8	368	4	17	423	4
9	404	4	18	381	4
Out	3,309	36	In	3,220	36
TOTALS				6,529	72

THE BELFRY

HOME OF THE PGA, the Belfry has become one of the best-known courses in Britain in recent years thanks largely to the mass of publicity given to the two Ryder Cup matches played there in the 1980s.

The first was in 1985 when Tony Jacklin and his gallant men became the first to beat the Americans since 1957 and then four years later they retained the trophy after a thrilling tie.

The Belfry was designed to be the British equivalent of Augusta, home of the US Masters. And whilst it certainly boasts some beautifully scenic holes, and attractive plantlife, it has not quite recaptured the beauty of Augusta, although it is a very good second.

It was transformed from potato fields to top-class golf course by designers Dave Thomas and Peter Alliss, and in 1977 it opened its doors for the first time. There are two courses, the Derby Course and the larger Brabazon Course which is used for major events.

The designers, in an attempt to give it a more American look, ensured that water became a major feature. And the 18th hole is one of the most picturesque in British golf. It requires two shots over water to the pin 474 yards away. The 10th is also very Americanized with the green being guarded by a large lake. The big hitters can reach the green off the tee. The not-so-big, and not-so-fortunate hitters, give their balls an "early bath".

The Hennessy Cognac Cup was the first major tournament at the Belfry, and the State Express Classic and Lawrence Batley Classic also had their homes at this West Midlands course situated near Sutton Coldfield. The English Open is now played there annually.

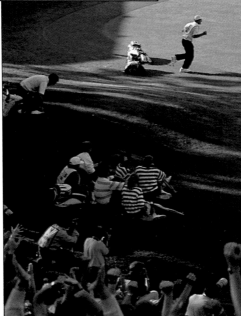

Top The Belfry Clubhouse. One of the finest English courses, the Belfry is now the home of the PGA.

Above The vast crowds bask in sunshine and glory as the Europeans retained the Ryder Cup after drawing 14-14 in 1989.

Left The Belfry's 10th has shades of Augusta about it with water being a prominent feature.

The Belfry Brabazon Course

DID YOU KNOW?

Golfing lore says that the word "fore" is believed to come from the military command "Beware before!" that was used in the 16th century to warn soldiers to fall to the ground to enable friendly gunfire to pass over them. It is believed that the Scottish reformer John Knox first used the term in the 16th century.

SCORECARD					
Hole	Yards	Par	Hole	Yards	Par
1	418	4	10	275	4
2	349	4	11	420	4
3	465	4	12	235	3
4	579	5	13	394	4
5	399	4	14	194	3
6	396	4	15	550	5
7	183	3	16	410	4
8	460	5	17	575	5
9	400	4	18	474	4
Out	3,649	37	In	3,527	36
TOTALS				7,176	73

ROYAL BIRKDALE

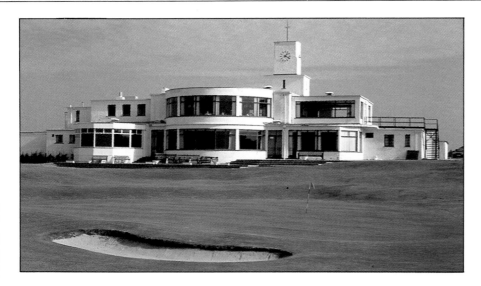

The impressive Royal Birkdale clubhouse.

WITH ITS SPLENDID clubhouse, the Royal Birkdale course on the outskirts of Southport is the finest and best-known course on that part of the Fylde coast, between the Merseyside town and Formby just down the coast.

Birkdale's severe rough makes it a testing course and one that calls for maximum effort from even the most qualified of players. It is regarded as one of the great modern-day championship courses.

The Birkdale club was founded by local enthusiasts in 1889 at a site closer to the town centre, with the Portland Hotel as its headquarters. But it moved to its present-day home about four miles from the town centre in 1897. It underwent major redesign work in 1931 and the clubhouse proudly stands as one of the finest in Britain.

The club was granted Royal patronage in 1951 and three years later it staged its first British Open, when Peter Thomson of Australia triumphed. It has now staged seven Opens, 1991 being the latest occasion that the Championship came to the north-west of England.

Although it has hosted championship golf since before the First World War it was not until after the Second World War that it hosted major international competitions. It has since hosted the Walker Cup, the Curtis Cup and the Ryder Cup, when Britain and the United States fought out a memorable tie here in 1969.

One of the British Open's great golf shots was played from behind a bush by Arnold Palmer at Birkdale's 15th hole (now 16th) on his way to winning his first title in 1961. Despite his lie, he found the green 140 yards away with a six-iron and was left with a 15-foot putt. A plaque has been laid into the fairway close to the spot where he played the magical shot.

The rough and bracken alongside the fairways give an appearance of severity, but it would be accurate to describe the course as "demanding but fair". However, play a wayward shot and it then becomes severe.

SCORECARD					
Hole	Yards	Par	Hole	Yards	Par
1	448	4	10	395	4
2	417	4	11	409	4
3	409	4	12	184	3
4	203	3	13	475	4
5	346	4	14	199	3
6	473	4	15	543	5
7	156	3	16	414	4
8	458	4	17	525	5
9	414	4	18	472	4
Out	3,324	34	In	3,616	36
TOTALS				6,940	70

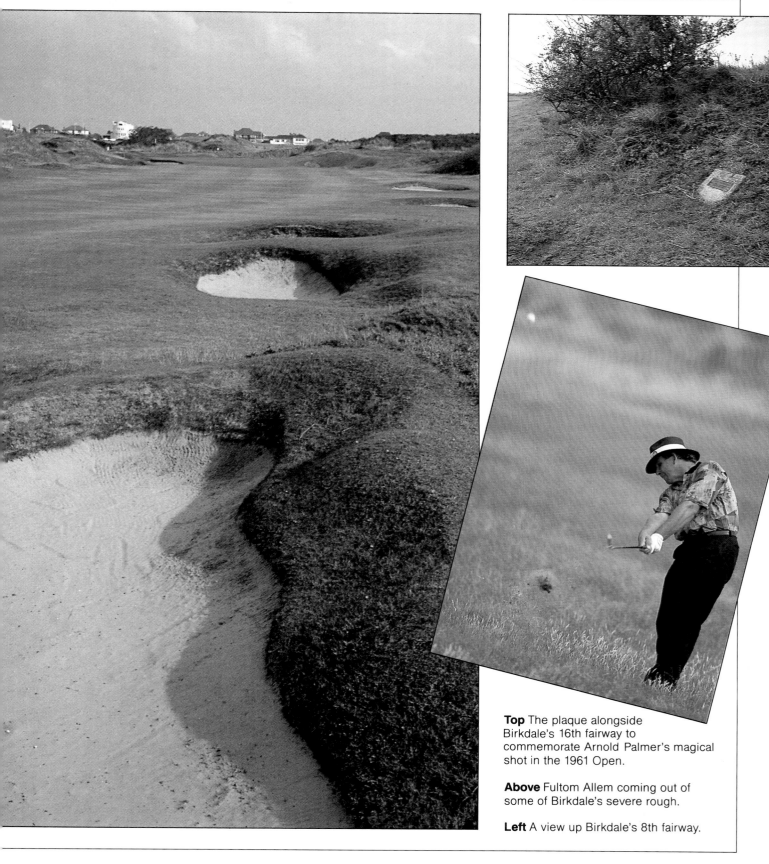

Top The plaque alongside Birkdale's 16th fairway to commemorate Arnold Palmer's magical shot in the 1961 Open.

Above Fultom Allem coming out of some of Birkdale's severe rough.

Left A view up Birkdale's 8th fairway.

ROYAL LIVERPOOL

THE ROYAL LIVERPOOL club is not situated in Liverpool, as its name implies, but is on the Wirral peninsula at Hoylake.

The club is steeped in golfing history and, apart from producing such great champions as John Ball and Harold Hilton, it was responsible for inaugurating many of the great championships which are still in existence today.

It played host to the first Amateur Championship in 1885, the first English Amateur Championship in 1925, was the venue for the first international match between England and Scotland in 1902, and the first between amateurs of Great Britain and the United States in 1921. This was the forerunner of the Walker Cup. Hardly surprisingly, with such a tradition, it has also been home of the British Open ten times between 1897 and 1967. Coincidentally, the first winner at Hoylake was the local amateur Harold Hilton.

The club was formed in 1869 by an exiled Scot living in the Liverpool area who laid out the course on a racecourse owned by the Royal Liverpool Hunt Club. After Westward Ho! it is the oldest English seaside course. Jack Morris, nephew of Old Tom

Morris, was the club's first professional. The course was increased to its full 18 holes in 1871 and has changed very little since. Many out-of-bounds markers await those wayward shots. The 11th hole is named the Alps because it has high sandhills which require a very long carry from the tee.

Right The clubhouse at the Royal Liverpool club, Hoylake.

Below Greg Norman in action at Hoylake's 11th.

	SCORECARD				
Hole	Yards	Par	Hole	Yards	Par
1	428	4	10	409	4
2	429	4	11	200	3
3	505	5	12	454	4
4	195	3	13	157	3
5	449	4	14	516	5
6	423	4	15	460	4
7	200	3	16	560	5
8	519	5	17	418	4
9	393	4	18	395	4
Out	3,541	36	In	3,569	36
TOTALS				7,110	72

ROYAL LYTHAM AND ST ANNES

THE FYLDE COAST course at Lytham first hosted the British Open in 1926 and was privileged to witness the great American amateur Bobby Jones win his first title. But for sheer nostalgia the 1969 Open took some beating: Tony Jacklin thwarted the challenge of the left-handed New Zealander Bob Charles to become the first British winner since Max Faulkner in 1951.

Lytham has a remarkable record of not having produced an American professional winner of the British Open despite staging the Championship eight times. Since Jones' victory the other winners, apart from Jacklin, have been Bobby Locke (South Africa), Peter Thomson (Australia), Bob Charles (New Zealand), Gary Player (South Africa) and Severiano Ballesteros (Spain) twice.

The original links were laid out in 1886 and ten years later they moved the small distance to their present site. It was designated a "Royal" course in 1926. The first championship at Lytham was the 1893 British Ladies.

Lytham is flat compared to some of the Scottish links but the wind that blows in from the Fylde estuary makes it as tough as any of

its Scottish rivals. And it demands complete accuracy off the tee, as Gary Player confirmed by using a one iron as opposed to a wood when he won the Open in 1974. Any lapse in concentration is severely punished by the hidden dangers of Lytham's links. The closing two holes, while not the severest in championship golf, can pose problems if concentration goes at that crucial time. Jack Nicklaus will bear that out because he needed two par fours at those holes to capture his first Open in 1963. He took fives.

Large crowds flock around Lytham's 18th hole, a great Championship closing hole.

SCORECARD					
Hole	Yards	Par	Hole	Yards	Par
1	206	3	10	334	4
2	420	4	11	485	5
3	458	4	12	189	3
4	393	4	13	339	4
5	188	3	14	445	4
6	486	5	15	468	4
7	551	5	16	356	4
8	394	4	17	413	4
9	162	3	18	386	4
Out	3,258	35	In	3,415	36
TOTALS				6,673	71

ROYAL ST GEORGE'S

THE ST GEORGE'S club was founded in 1887 and seven years later it became the first English course to stage the British Open. Between then and 1949 it played host to the world's greatest tournament ten times. But the facilities and amenities at nearby Sandwich were becoming inadequate for the vast army of fans flocking to the Open in those post-war years and it was removed from the Open roster until making a welcome return in 1981. Four years later Sandwich was to witness the first British success in "her" Open for 16 years when Sandy Lyle beat the world.

St George's is a very undulating course and to have one leg three or four inches shorter than the other would be a great advantage. Large bunkers and the wind are additional hazards.

St George's has witnessed some memorable moments, and there was none finer than Tony Jacklin performing the first-ever televised hole-in-one in Britain during the 1967 Dunlop Masters, when he did so at the short 16th. And it was at St George's in 1922 that the flamboyant Walter Hagen became the first American-born winner of

the British Open. That was the start of a domination that has more or less lasted 70 years. The great Bobby Jones led the Americans to victory in the first Walker Cup match to be played in England in 1930, and four years later it was Britain's Henry Cotton

who set St George's alight with blistering rounds of 67 and 65 as he captured the first of his three Open titles.

The triangle of holes constituting the 13th, 14th and 15th in the far corner of the course are where rounds are made or broken. Each of the three greens at those holes is surrounded by bunkers. But survive those three and the homeward run is not too difficult.

Royal St George's Old Course

SCORECARD					
Hole	Yards	Par	Hole	Yards	Par
1	445	4	10	399	4
2	376	4	11	216	3
3	214	3	12	362	4
4	470	4	13	443	4
5	422	4	14	508	5
6	156	3	15	467	4
7	529	5	16	165	3
8	415	4	17	425	4
9	387	4	18	458	4
Out	3,414	35	In	3,443	35
TOTALS				6,857	70

Many of the great English courses are ringed with expensive houses. St George's is no exception.

SUNNINGDALE

SITUATED IN BERKSHIRE, the Sunningdale golf club, with its Old and New courses, provides some of the finest golf in southern England.

Founded in 1900 the Old course was laid out by Willie Park and the New course, designed by Harry Colt, was completed in 1922. A prestigious club, it has been honoured to have two Royal captains over the years with Edward VIII filling that role when he was the Prince of Wales, and George VI taking up the captaincy when he was the Duke of York.

While the Old course has been used for some major events over the years, like the Dunlop Masters, and as a qualifying venue for the British Open, it is a bit too small for major championships. However, the popular Sunningdale Foursomes have been held there since 1934. And since 1982, the European Open has been staged at Sunningdale eight times.

Gary Player won his first ever British professional tournament, the Dunlop Tournament, at Sunningdale in 1956, when he shot a course record 64. The record was lowered to 61 by Peter Butler during the 1967 Bowmaker Tournament.

Sunningdale is one of England's finest golf courses. However, because of its location it is not an Open Championship venue.

Sunningdale New Course

SCORECARD

Hole	Yards	Par	Hole	Yards	Par
1	466	4	10	213	3
2	175	3	11	453	4
3	396	4	12	400	4
4	436	4	13	553	5
5	190	3	14	194	3
6	492	5	15	446	4
7	383	4	16	385	4
8	402	4	17	175	3
9	440	4	18	477	5
Out	3,380	35	In	3,296	35
TOTALS				6,676	70

WENTWORTH

SITUATED AT VIRGINIA Water, Surrey, Wentworth is one of England's best-known courses and has been used for major championships since its opening in 1924. It has not staged the British Open, though, because it is not a links course.

The East Course was the first to be opened and it was followed by the West Course in the 1930s. But it was not until after the war that the latter became established as Wentworth's championship course. Because of its length, nearly 7,000 yards, it was nicknamed the "Burma Road". And its par-5 17th, with its dogleg left, is one of the game's great long holes - a view confirmed by Arnold Palmer.

The home of the World Matchplay Championship every year, Wentworth has also played host to all the great team competitions including the Ryder Cup and Canada Cup (now the World Cup). The forerunner of the Ryder Cup, a match between British and American professionals, was held at Wentworth in 1926. The Volvo PGA Championship, one of the top PGA European Tour events, is played at Wentworth each year and, because of its close location to London, it is a very popular course for pro-am and celebrity events. The course has undergone many changes in the last 20 years.

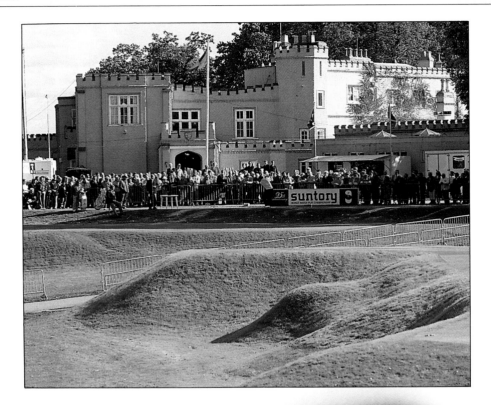

The clubhouse at Wentworth, Virginia Water, Surrey.

Wentworth West Course

SCORECARD					
Hole	Yards	Par	Hole	Yards	Par
1	471	5	10	186	3
2	155	3	11	376	4
3	452	4	12	483	5
4	501	5	13	441	4
5	191	3	14	179	3
6	344	4	15	466	4
7	399	4	16	380	4
8	398	4	17	571	5
9	450	4	18	502	5
Out	3,361	36	In	3,584	37
TOTALS				6,945	73

Above Nick Faldo driving at one of Wentworth's tree-lined fairways. On this occasion it is also 'spectator-lined'.

Left A large gallery skirts the green at Wentworth's 18th during the 1989 PGA Championship won by Nick Faldo.

CHANTILLY

NOT ONLY IS Chantilly one of the oldest golf courses in France but it is also one of the finest.

Dating from 1908, it has staged the French Open many times, the first being in 1913 when George Duncan took the title.

Situated 25 miles (40km) north of Paris it is a typical shrubland course set amidst woodland. Its 6,500 metres offer one of the most testing of challenges in Europe.

The present-day championship course was designed by Tom Simpson in the 1920s, but much of his good work was ruined by World War II bombs. Despite being rebuilt, much of his original design remains. Three of the four par-3s are over 183 metres long which make its par-71 one of the toughest to achieve.

Although set in woodland, it has been designed to give ample room to play golf without having

The impressive Chantilly clubhouse.

to worry constantly about the trees. But the enclosure created by the trees gives an atmosphere of isolation and there are no distractions from the job in hand.

Britain's Peter Oosterhuis won the French Open at Chantilly in 1974. The next time Chantilly hosted the championship in 1988 it was another Briton, Nick Faldo, who captured the title. And at the same venue 12 months later he made it back-to-back victories.

SCORECARD					
Hole	Metres	Par	Hole	Metres	Par
1	418	4	10	434	4
2	362	4	11	389	4
3	158	3	12	368	4
4	358	4	13	418	4
5	397	4	14	199	3
6	198	3	15	381	4
7	401	4	16	193	3
8	527	5	17	392	4
9	459	5	18	545	5
Out	3,278	36	In	3,319	35
TOTALS				6,597	71

St Nom-la-Breteche

THE ST NOM-LA-BRETECHE is situated 15 miles from Paris close to Versailles. The original course was laid out by the British designer Fred Hawtree.

It has three times been used for the French Open, the first being in 1965 when Ramon Sota of Spain shot a course record 62. When it was last held there in 1982 it was won by Sota's nephew, Severiano Ballesteros.

The Versailles course has played host to the end-of-season Lancôme Trophy since it was first held in 1970.

There are two other courses at St Nom-la-Breteche, the Red and Blue.

SCORECARD

Hole	Metres	Par	Hole	Metres	Par
1	333	4	10	382	4
2	381	4	11	341	4
3	173	3	12	498	5
4	363	4	13	196	3
5	444	5	14	325	4
6	400	4	15	362	4
7	465	5	16	175	3
8	386	4	17	465	5
9	191	3	18	332	4
Out	3,136	36	In	3,076	36
TOTALS				6,212	72

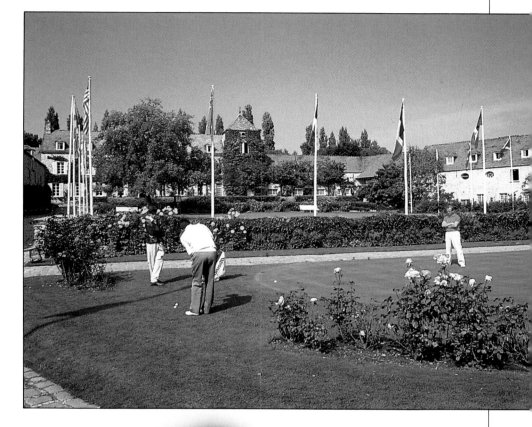

Players practise their putting before the 1989 Lancôme Trophy at St Nom-la-Breteche.

DID YOU KNOW?

An estimated 300 million golf balls are sold worldwide each year.

ROYAL COUNTY DOWN

THE SETTING OF the Royal County Down course, some 30 miles south of Belfast, makes it one of Ireland's truly picturesque courses. The backdrop of the Mountains of Mourne and the shores of Dundrum Bay make it one of the great seaside courses. The club was formed in 1889 and the committee recruited the services of Tom Morris to lay out the course at a cost of "not more than £4". It doesn't seem much, but Tom managed it, thanks largely to the wonderful natural resources the area offered.

It received Royal patronage in 1908 when it stood proudly as one of the finest courses in the British Isles.

John Ball won the first national championship to be played at County Down in 1893 and five years later the first professional tournament was won by Harry Vardon, who was a great lover of the Ulster course. Vardon loved it so much that day that he beat his great rival J H Taylor 12 and 11.

While the course would do justice to a major championship

like the British Open, the lack of nearby qualifying courses and accommodation means it has been overlooked. But who knows? Royal County Down could just become the second Irish course to stage the Open Championship.

Right Royal County Down on a grey and murky day with the backdrop of the Mountains of Mourne.

SCORECARD					
Hole	Yards	Par	Hole	Yards	Par
1	506	5	10	200	3
2	424	4	11	440	4
3	473	4	12	501	5
4	217	3	13	445	4
5	440	4	14	213	3
6	396	4	15	445	4
7	145	3	16	265	4
8	427	4	17	400	4
9	486	5	18	545	5
Out	3,514	36	In	3,454	36
TOTALS				6,968	72

ROYAL PORTRUSH

ROYAL PORTRUSH HOLDS a special place in British Open history because it is the only Irish course to play host to the world's greatest tournament. That was back in 1951 when Britain's Max Faulkner captured the title.

Founded in 1888 Portrush, with its three courses, is steeped in history and tradition. The best known of the courses is the championship Dunluce course. Originally known as the Country Club, Portrush was granted Royal patronage by the Duke of York in 1892, and in 1895 it became the Royal Portrush Golf Club with the Prince of Wales as patron.

Originally a nine-hole course, a second nine were added within a year. Changes over the years have resulted in many holes moving outwards towards the sand dunes, thus making it as severe a test as any links course in the British Isles.

The fairways on the Dunluce course are all narrow and with the exception of the first and last holes, are doglegged. The 11th, because of its location, can be anything from a medium iron to a full-blooded wood off the tee, depending upon which way the wind is blowing.

Left A view across the Portrush course with the town in the background.

SCORECARD					
Hole	Yards	Par	Hole	Yards	Par
1	389	4	10	480	5
2	497	5	11	166	3
3	159	3	12	395	4
4	455	4	13	371	4
5	384	4	14	213	3
6	193	3	15	366	4
7	432	4	16	432	4
8	376	4	17	517	5
9	476	5	18	481	5
Out	3,361	36	In	3,421	37
TOTALS				6,782	73

Left Action at Royal Portrush's 11th. It remains the only Irish course to host the British Open.

Royal Portrush Dunluce Course

PENINA

SITUATED IN THE Algarve, that popular golfing area of Portugal, Penina was designed on bare flat fields by one of Britain's best-loved golfers, Henry Cotton, in 1964.

More than a quarter-of-a-million trees and shrubs transformed the bare land into a beautiful golf course. Cotton set up his home at Penina and spent much of his later life in the Algarve sun.

Cotton designed the course as only a champion could. It is long and each shot must be planned in advance. Haste is a foolhardy gamble at Penina. Time and pre-planning are two important essentials when playing the 6,439-metre course.

Henry Cotton used the course for his golfing school and the PGA Tour has continued the tradition by taking young hopefuls to that area of Portugal each year for a coaching programme. Cotton may no longer be with us but his dream certainly is.

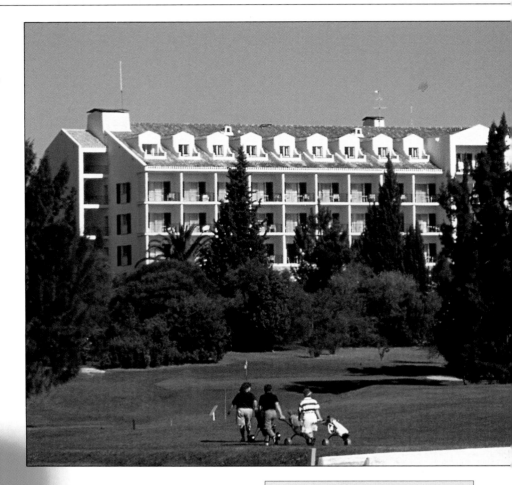

SCORECARD					
Hole	Metres	Par	Hole	Metres	Par
1	411	4	10	500	5
2	401	4	11	491	5
3	301	4	12	397	4
4	375	4	13	208	3
5	463	5	14	394	4
6	186	3	15	318	4
7	299	4	16	210	3
8	180	3	17	450	5
9	405	4	18	450	5
Out	3,021	35	In	3,418	38
TOTALS				6,439	73

DID YOU KNOW?

On 12 December 1899, George Grant was issued patent number 638,920 for the golf tee.

Left The Penina Hotel dominates the background at Portugal's best known course.

Below The great climate and sun help make the Penina setting even more beautiful.

CARNOUSTIE

WHEN USED FOR the British Open in 1968 Carnoustie's course, at 7,252 yards, became the longest ever in Open history. It was first used for the Championship in 1931, when Tommy Armour of America was the winner. It has been used five times in all, the last being in 1975 when Tom Watson beat the luckless Australian Jack Newton to win his first title.

The course held no fear for Ben Hogan, who won three of the four Majors in 1953 including the Open. Even the monster par-five 6th didn't bother him, and he twice birdied the hole on the last day in winning the title.

Built on public ground at Angus, the club was founded in 1842. Many natural hazards make the course difficult and the closing three holes are probably the toughest in championship golf in Britain. The 235-yard par-3 16th requires only the best of tee shots and the last two, the Island and Home holes, each require the Barry Burn to be negotiated. Jockie's Burn zig-zags its way across the course and adds to the problems at four of the first six holes.

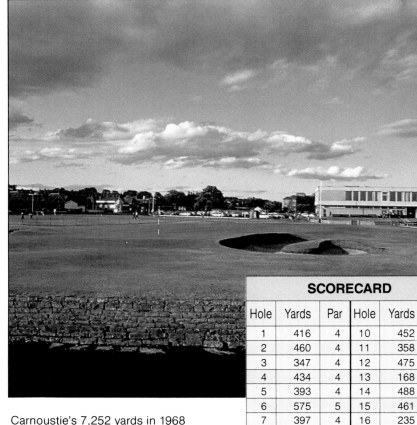

Carnoustie's 7,252 yards in 1968 makes it the longest course ever used for the British Open.

SCORECARD

Hole	Yards	Par	Hole	Yards	Par
1	416	4	10	452	4
2	460	4	11	358	4
3	347	4	12	475	5
4	434	4	13	168	3
5	393	4	14	488	5
6	575	5	15	461	4
7	397	4	16	235	3
8	183	3	17	455	4
9	474	4	18	486	4
Out	3,679	36	In	3,578	36
TOTALS				7,252	72

GLENEAGLES

BECAUSE IT IS not a links course, Gleneagles has never staged the British Open. Nevertheless it is one of the most beautiful courses in Britain and is steeped in tradition.

Two of the world's most famous golfers designed the three championship courses at The Gleneagles Hotel. James Braid, five times winner of the Open championship, designed the King's and Queen's at the beginning of the century and now the great Jack Nicklaus has designed the Monarch's.

The original design of the King's and Queen's represents some of the finest examples of "classical" golf course design. The King's is outward looking and the Queen's predominantly inward. The Monarch's, best described as a "modern classic"; is a combination of both.

Home of the Bell's Scottish Open, the King's Course has a traditional Scottish layout described as "straight out and straight in". The fairways are generous in width and the greens large, approximately 600 square metres. The magnificent course offers the golfer a real challenge, especially on the last few holes, where the 17th runs into the wind after playing the previous 4 holes downwind. In return it provides breathtaking vistas of hillsides, moorland and glens, amongst which the hotel is set.

The beautiful Queen's is generally considered easier than the King's. Essentially it requires shorter second shots to the greens and the good bunkering provides a demanding test for the golfer. The course typifies the "Gleneagles golfing experience" with a design which tests the golfer, combined with stunning scenery.

People come to Gleneagles to stay at the famous Gleneagles Hotel, as well as to play golf; both are spectacular.

Gleneagles King's Course

SCORECARD

Hole	Yards	Par	Hole	Yards	Par
1	362	4	10	447	4
2	405	4	11	230	3
3	374	4	12	395	4
4	466	4	13	448	4
5	161	3	14	260	4
6	476	5	15	459	4
7	439	4	16	135	3
8	158	3	17	377	4
9	354	4	18	525	5
Out	3,195	35	In	3,276	35
TOTALS				6,471	70

111

MUIRFIELD

AFTER LEAVING THEIR Musselburgh home, the Honourable Company of Edinburgh Golfers took up their new home at Muirfield in 1892.

Situated on the shores of the Firth of Forth, the famous course has played host to the British Open 14 times, with the 1992 Championship being held there to mark the 100th anniversary of Muirfield's first Open, which was won by Harold Hilton, an Englishman.

Muirfield's near-7,000 yard course is a very testing one and is a "true" championship course. The world's leading professionals have nothing but the utmost respect for it.

Being on the Firth of Forth one of the big problems at Muirfield, like all links courses, is the wind.

Right Muirfield's 13th green.

Below One of Muirfield's bunkers in the foreground with the clubhouse in the background.

SCORECARD					
Hole	Yards	Par	Hole	Yards	Par
1	447	4	10	475	4
2	351	4	11	385	4
3	379	4	12	381	4
4	180	3	13	159	3
5	559	5	14	449	4
6	469	4	15	417	4
7	185	3	16	188	3
8	444	4	17	550	5
9	504	5	18	448	4
Out	3,518	36	In	3,452	35
TOTALS				6,970	71

Few holes run in the same direction so it is difficult to keep track of the wind. The narrow fairways and the relatively small greens add further to Muirfield's severity. And the two closing holes are amongst the sternest in championship golf, demanding the most accurate of tee shots.

But the best names in golf have beaten both wind and course to capture the Open at Muirfield. There was Henry Cotton's brilliant display of driving in 1948, Gary Player in 1959 when he won his first Open, and Jack Nicklaus beating the severe rough to take his first title in 1966. Nicklaus later named his own course in Ohio after the famous Scottish links. And for sheer magic there was Lee Trevino's chip at the 71st hole which went into the cup and destroyed Tony Jacklin's chances of a second British Open title. They were all memorable Open occasions at Muirfield.

It has also staged other leading tournaments, including all the top amateur events, and in 1973 the Ryder Cup was played north of the border for the one and only time at Muirfield's famous links.

Muirfield has a big advantage over some other championship courses; it is a great spectator course offering many fine vantage points. Consequently it remains very much part of the British Open roster.

PRESTWICK

AYRSHIRE'S PRESTWICK COURSE is no longer the great championship course it was. But its place in British Open history should never be forgotten.

The very first major championship in the world, the British Open, was played over Prestwick's 12-hole links in 1860, and the famous course staged every championship up to 1872, thereafter sharing it with Musselburgh and St Andrews.

Golf had been played at Prestwick for many years before the course was laid out on common land in 1851. The splendid sea-washed turf made it a very attractive course to play on in those days and the small greens set amongst undulating hollows made it a severe test for the best of golfers, like Allan Robertson.

And it was after Robertson's death that the Prestwick club organized the first Open championship to find his successor as "champion golfer of the four Kingdoms".

Three rounds of Prestwick's 12 holes made up the first Open, won by Willie Park of Musselburgh. It became an 18-hole course in 1883 and the first Amateur Championship was held at Prestwick in 1888. Over the following years it became established as one of the great championship courses.

However, in the years after the First World War, and with the new breed of American professional making the trip across the Atlantic for the Open each year, it was no longer the severe test it used to be, and the two short closing holes were far too easy for such an event. Furthermore its geographic location made it a difficult course

for spectators to reach and in 1925 Prestwick staged its last British Open.

However, the Amateur Championship continued to be played at Prestwick until the

The famous Cardinal Bunker which makes Prestwick's par-5 third hole even more testing.

1950s. It remained very much a male stronghold and did not even have ladies' tees until installing them for the 1978 Scottish Ladies' Championship.

Despite no longer being a major championship course, Prestwick remains a crucial stopping off point for golfers who make annual trips to the famous Scottish courses, as they have not forgotten its place in golfing history.

SCORECARD					
Hole	Yards	Par	Hole	Yards	Par
1	346	4	10	454	4
2	167	3	11	195	3
3	482	5	12	513	5
4	382	4	13	460	4
5	206	3	14	362	4
6	362	4	15	347	4
7	430	4	16	288	4
8	431	4	17	391	4
9	444	4	18	284	4
Out	3,250	35	In	3,294	36
TOTALS				6,544	71

ROYAL DORNOCH

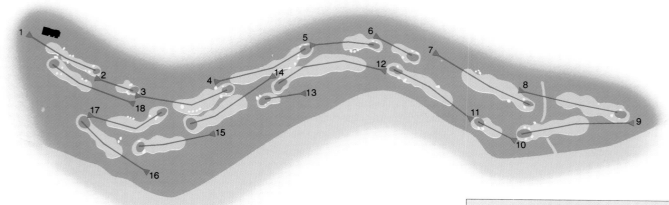

SCORECARD

Hole	Yards	Par	Hole	Yards	Par
1	332	4	10	150	3
2	182	3	11	445	4
3	413	4	12	516	5
4	418	4	13	168	3
5	357	4	14	445	4
6	164	3	15	323	4
7	463	4	16	400	4
8	437	4	17	410	4
9	497	5	18	461	4
Out	3,263	35	In	3,318	35
TOTALS				6,581	70

ROYAL DORNOCH IS the most northerly first-class golf course in Britain. Situated on the south-east coast of Sutherland there are two courses, with the Old course being the most famous.

Because of the Gulf Stream, golf is played all the year round without the problems that the winter months bring to other British courses. And had it been located in a more accessible part of Scotland it would almost certainly have served as an Open venue because it is a true links course and those who have played it will testify to its acceptability as a championship venue.

Golf was played at Dornoch in the early 17th century although the Dornoch Golf Club was not founded until 1877. A few years later Tom Morris senior was commissioned to lay out a nine-hole course.

It soon became an 18-hole course and under the direction of John Sutherland, secretary of the club for 50 years, it was elevated to a championship-rated course in 1904. In the pre-war years all the leading professionals of the day made a point of playing exhibition and money matches at Dornoch. And it was Vardon who described the 14th as the finest natural golf hole he had ever played.

Small, well-guarded greens make Dornoch a demanding course and, of course, the variable wind offered by its location makes it as difficult as any links course.

The spectacular setting of Britain's most northerly first class golf course, Royal Dornoch.

ROYAL TROON

UNDULATING FAIRWAYS AND severe rough make Troon one of the most testing of British championship courses.

Situated north of Ayr on the west coast of Scotland, six of Troon's holes run alongside the Firth of Clyde and, as such, wind poses the biggest problem. They are said to be so severe at times that fish have been washed up on the greens!

The club was founded in 1878 and was first added to the British Open list of courses in 1923 when Archie Havers won. The second Open here was not until after the war, when South African Bobby Locke captured the title. It has been used four more times, the last being in 1989 when America's Mark Calcavecchia was the surprise winner after a play-off.

Arnold Palmer lowered the 72-hole British Open record to 276 at Troon when winning his second successive title in 1962, and 11 years later Tom Weiskopf equalled the record.

The longest hole in Open history was Troon's 577-yard 6th and, strangely, the shortest was

also at Troon - the notorious Postage Stamp hole (8th) measured 126 yards in 1973. And it was at the Postage Stamp that 71-year-old Gene Sarazen holed-in-one in front of the television cameras during that year. But don't remind German amateur Herman Tissies about the Postage Stamp - he took 15 strokes during the 1950 Open.

Troon was granted Royal status in its centenary year, 1978.

Below Tom Kite playing to one of Britain's best known holes, Troon's 8th, the 'Postage Stamp'.

Bottom left Fans enthralled by the action during the 1989 Open at Troon which provided a surprise winner, Mark Calcavecchia of the United States.

SCORECARD					
Hole	Yards	Par	Hole	Yards	Par
1	364	4	10	438	4
2	391	4	11	481	5
3	379	4	12	431	4
4	557	5	13	465	4
5	210	3	14	179	3
6	577	5	15	457	4
7	402	4	16	542	5
8	126	3	17	223	3
9	423	4	18	452	4
Out	3,429	36	In	3,668	36
TOTALS				7,097	72

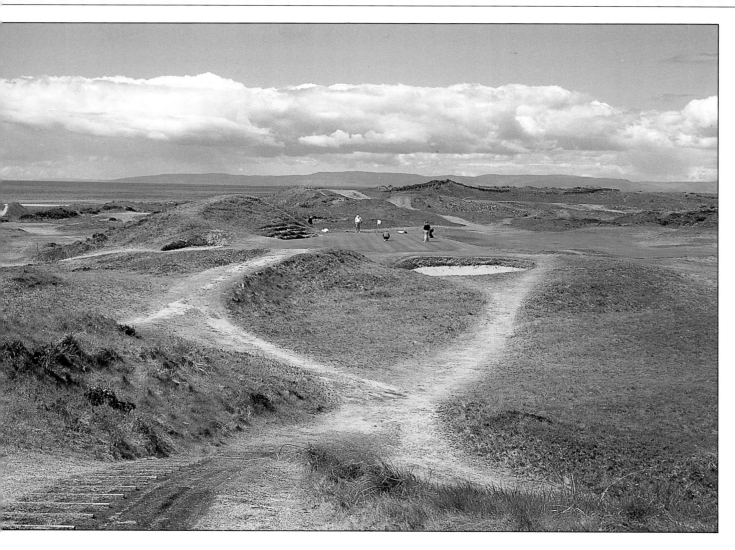

A view of the 'Postage Stamp' from tee to pin. It was at this hole in 1973 that 71-year-old Gene Sarazen holed-in-one during the Open.

ST ANDREWS

ST ANDREWS IS regarded as the "home" of golf. And why not? Golf has been played in the Burgh since the 16th century, and probably earlier.

The first record of golf at St Andrews was in 1552, but it is safe to assume it was played there some years earlier and possibly in 1457 when King James II banned the playing of golf because it interfered with archery practice.

The Society of St Andrews Golfers was formed at a meeting on 12 May 1754. The site of the original club house is unknown, but it is known that the members used to fill themselves with food and drink at Baillie Glass's before moving on to the Union Parlour. The present clubhouse was erected in 1854, one hundred years after the formation of the Society. Twenty years earlier, in 1834, the club had changed its name to the Royal and Ancient Golf Club (R & A) after King William IV agreed to become the club's first patron. Captaincy of the R & A remains

one of the game's greatest honours.

The R & A gained in popularity towards the end of the 19th century, and after more and more clubs turned to them for clarification on rules of the game they officially became the governing authority on the rules in 1897.

The original St Andrews course, alongside St Andrews Bay, was a 22-hole course but had only 12 huge greens. Players started alongside the home hole (22nd) and played 11 holes out before turning and playing the same holes again but in the opposite direction.

The first four holes were later reduced to two, which cut down the number of greens to ten and the holes to 18. However, golf became dangerous with sets of players hitting balls in opposite directions. It was therefore necessary to widen the fairways and cut two holes into each green. And the double-holed greens remain a feature of the Old

Course. Today there are eleven greens, seven of them double greens.

A second course, the New Course, was added in 1894. The Jubilee course was completed in 1897 and in 1912 the Eden Course, required to meet the increased demands, was completed.

It was anticipated in the early days that golf would be free to all at St Andrews, but such was the demand that green fees were eventually charged for the first time in 1913.

The Old Course is the one that is used for all major championships, and it staged the first of its record-equalling 24 British Opens in 1873. In the early days of championship golf many champions came from St Andrews.

Far left The St Andrews clubhouse.

Left The 17th at St Andrews, the 'Road Hole'.

Below Mark James playing to the 'Road Hole'.

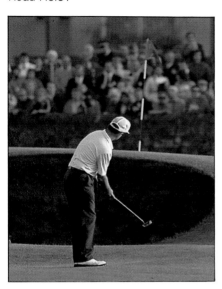

SCORECARD					
Hole	Yards	Par	Hole	Yards	Par
1	370	4	10	342	4
2	411	4	11	172	3
3	371	4	12	316	4
4	463	4	13	425	4
5	564	5	14	567	5
6	416	4	15	413	4
7	372	4	16	382	4
8	178	3	17	461	4
9	356	4	18	354	4
Out	3,501	36	In	3,432	36
TOTALS				6,933	72

Notably there was Andrew Strath and Old and Young Tom Morris.

Apart from its double greens, a major feature of St Andrews is the many huge bunkers, including the Hell bunker, which awaits any wayward shot on the 14th. And many great golfers have flirted with trouble in the Hell bunker over the years.

The Road Hole, the 17th, is a 461-yard par-4, but can prove to be one of the most difficult in world golf. Many great rounds have fallen apart at this one hole. And for sheer excitement, the walk up the 18th fairway to the last green with the magnificent clubhouse in front of you is one of the great moments in golf.

TURNBERRY

WITH THE BEAUTIFUL backdrop of the Ailsa Craig and Isle of Arran, Turnberry has one of the finest settings of all championship courses in Britain.

Golf was played at Turnberry in the last century when the Marquis of Ailsa had a private course on his Culzean estate. But it was not until 1903 that the Turnberry Hotel Golf Club was founded. The second course was laid out between the two wars and the two courses were named the Ailsa and Arran courses. The Ailsa is the championship course used today.

Perhaps strangely, Turnberry was not used for its first British Open until 1977, when Tom Watson and Jack Nicklaus engaged in a great battle which saw British Open records tumble.

Because of its geographic location, Turnberry's links were requisitioned during both wars and during the Second World War were extensively damaged when used as runways by RAF Coastal Command. But it was thanks to the efforts of Frank Hole, and the skills of course architect Mackenzie Ross, that Turnberry was opened again in 1951.

Ross's "new" courses soon gained rave notices and in the early 1950s Turnberry was used for the Scottish National Championships. When the *News of the World* Matchplay Championship and Walker Cup were held there it was hailed as a great championship course. It eventually joined the list of British Open courses.

The Turnberry Hotel is popular with tourists, particularly the Japanese, and in 1987 the 133-room hotel and two courses passed into Japanese hands for $24 million.

SCORECARD					
Hole	Yards	Par	Hole	Yards	Par
1	350	4	10	452	4
2	428	4	11	177	3
3	462	4	12	448	4
4	167	3	13	411	4
5	441	4	14	440	4
6	222	3	15	209	3
7	528	5	16	409	4
8	427	4	17	500	5
9	455	4	18	431	4
Out	3,480	35	In	3,477	35
TOTALS				6,957	70

Above Turnberry offers not only the finest golf but also the best in hotels.

Above right The lighthouse is one of Turnberry's many natural features.

Right Action from the 1989 Senior Championship at Turnberry which was won by New Zealander Bob Charles.

Turnberry Ailsa Course

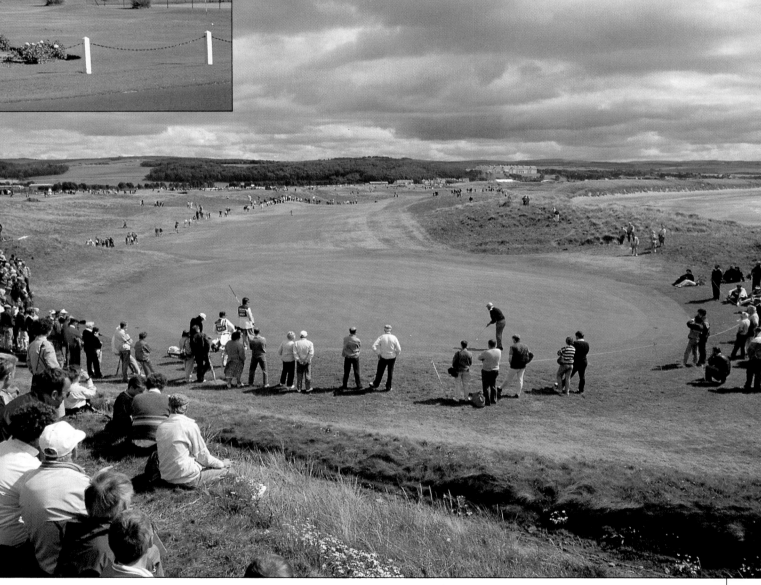

VALDERRAMA

SITUATED ON SPAIN'S Costa del Sol, Valderrama is rapidly gaining a reputation for being "Europe's Augusta".

Set among beautiful cork trees at Sotogrande, the course was originally laid out in 1964 by Robert Trent Jones and two years later it hosted the Spanish Open. That championship was won by Argentinian Roberto de Vicenzo who shot a second round 66, which included a three-putt from a mere five yards on the last green.

Formerly known as Los Aves, the course was acquired by a Spanish industrialist and a consortium of seven friends in 1985 who wanted to turn it into an exclusive private club but at the same time make it a challenging championship course. The latter was achieved when Jones was again called in to make the necessary changes. Its 6,353 metres, par 71, make Valderrama one of the great championship courses on the European Tour and the back nine holes rank among the toughest on the Tour.

Situated close to the Mediterranean, Valderrama offers not only a stiff challenge to any golfer, but also some wonderful panoramic views which can often distract the player from the job in hand . . . trying to conquer the course!

Valderrama has hosted the Volvo Masters since its inauguration in 1988 when Britain's Nick Faldo carried off the title.

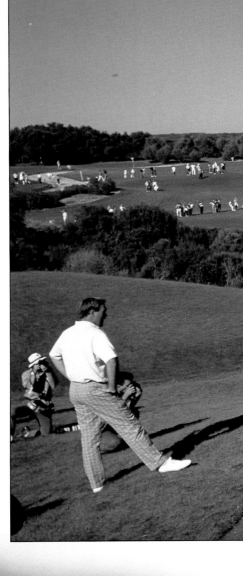

Right Jose-Maria Olazabal plays the 15th hole in the 1989 Volvo Masters.

Below right Beautiful and lush, Valderrama is an enchanting course.

SCORECARD

Hole	Metres	Par	Hole	Metres	Par
1	354	4	10	369	4
2	375	4	11	504	5
3	156	3	12	200	3
4	515	5	13	367	4
5	344	4	14	337	4
6	150	3	15	207	3
7	420	4	16	385	4
8	319	4	17	519	5
9	415	4	18	417	4
Out	3,048	35	In	3,305	36
TOTALS				6,353	71

CRANS-SUR-SIERRE

THE HOME OF the Swiss Open since 1939, the Crans-sur-Sierre Golf Club is situated 5,000 feet above the Rhône Valley and is overlooked by the Matterhorn. Its setting is spectacular.

The first Crans course was laid out by Sir Arnold Lunn, an international skiing pioneer, in 1905. He had already built the Palace Hotel, but the tourists never came as expected and the course closed during the war. Attempts to revive golf in the area were mooted in 1923 and in 1927 the current courses were opened. The rarified atmosphere helps the ball off the tee.

During the 1978 Open José-Maria Olazabal of Spain established a European record 27 strokes for nine holes and during the 1971 Open Italy's Baldovino Dassu established a European record of 60 for 18 holes. That record still stands today.

The course is covered in snow in the winter months, but when the snows have cleared it always comes back to its former glory. It is the largest club in Switzerland.

SCORECARD					
Hole	Metres	Par	Hole	Metres	Par
1	490	5	10	370	4
2	395	4	11	190	3
3	165	3	12	355	4
4	460	4	13	185	3
5	315	4	14	520	5
6	295	4	15	475	5
7	275	4	16	290	4
8	160	3	17	315	4
9	565	5	18	345	4
Out	3,120	36	In	3,045	36
TOTALS				6,165	72

The Crans-sur-Sierre course in the Rhône Valley is one of the most picturesque in Europe. Its setting in the shadow of the Matterhorn makes its location magnificent.

AUGUSTA

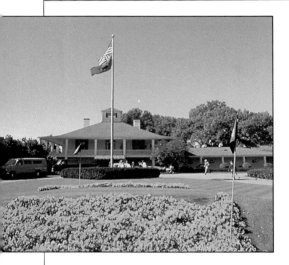

THE AUGUSTA NATIONAL course at Augusta, Georgia is, without doubt, one of *the* great golf courses of the world. For sheer beauty it has no rival.

The Augusta course, and the Masters, which has been played here since its launch in 1934, were the brainchild of locally-born Bobby Jones, who became one of the world's top golfers before his early retirement in 1930, and his great friend Clifford Roberts.

They recruited the services of top golf-course designer Alister Mackenzie, and in 1931 the dream of the Augusta National came to fruition. Jones decided to call it the Augusta *National* because the intention was to attract people from all over America to his beautiful new course.

Each hole is named after the tree, shrub or plant that lines the fairway and the names of the 18 holes are reminders of the days when the 385-acre site used to be a nursery. The names of the holes are as follows:

1	Tea Olive	10	Camellia
2	Pink Dogwood	11	White Dogwood
3	Flowering Peach	12	Golden Bell
4	Crab Apple	13	Azalea
5	Magnolia	14	Chinese Fir
6	Juniper	15	Firethorn
7	Pampas	16	Red Bud
8	Yellow Jasmine	17	Nandina
9	Carolina Cherry	18	Holly

The tall pine trees, often creating giant shadows across the course, are a major feature of Augusta. And the lakes offer not only beauty but a challenge to the very best of golfers. The lake in front of the 16th green has been the end of many a fine round.

Each hole must be pre-calculated, and playing on the putting surfaces requires the very best eye to read the greens - they have numerous twists, turns and rolls, and are among the fastest in the world. How many times have you seen a putt look like it's going into the hole at Augusta then roll away by feet, not inches?

Jones played each hole countless times before he decided on the placements of the greens and other features, and he knew when it was finished that only the best would conquer Augusta. But the one man to do so is Jack Nicklaus, who has won the coveted Masters green jacket six times.

The course has altered only slightly since Jones's original idea, although the front nine and back nine have now swapped places.

The turning point in so many rounds at Augusta comes at the Amen Corner, which is a name given to the 11th, 12th and 13th holes. They run alongside Rae's Creek and water awaits any shots off course.

Augusta is the only course to stage a Major every year, and it has seen some memorable moments since the inauguration of the Masters in 1934. And it was only one year old when Gene Sarazen had a remarkable double albatross two at the par-5 15th. It is still a much-talked-about golf shot down Georgia way. And in 1987, there was Larry Mize's chip at the second extra play-off hole, the 11th, from the rough 30 yards from the hole, to beat Greg Norman and capture his first Major.

The home of the Masters has seen some great moments, as befits the most beautiful golf course in the world.

Above left The Augusta clubhouse.

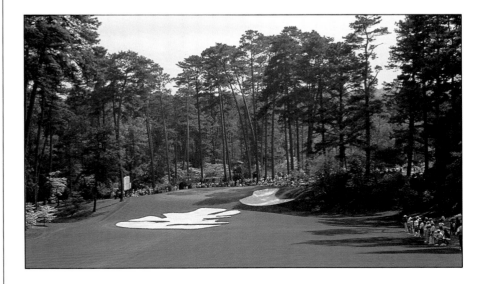

Left The 10th, just one of Augusta's many spectacular holes.

One of the features at Augusta is the water adjacent to many greens; the 16th is one such hole.

SCORECARD					
Hole	Yards	Par	Hole	Yards	Par
1	400	4	10	485	4
2	555	5	11	455	4
3	360	4	12	155	3
4	205	3	13	465	5
5	435	4	14	405	4
6	180	3	15	500	5
7	360	4	16	170	3
8	535	5	17	400	4
9	435	4	18	405	4
Out	3,465	36	In	3,440	36
TOTALS				6,905	72

BALTUSROL

ONE OF THE oldest golf clubs in America, Baltusrol is situated at Springfield, New Jersey. It was opened in 1895 and is named after a local farmer, Baltus Roll, who was murdered in 1825.

The course was laid out by Louis Keller, the owner and publisher of the *New York Social Register*. He owned the land at the foot of Baltusrol Mountain close to the New York State line.

It has played host to most leading American tournaments since it staged the US Ladies' Championship in 1901. It has hosted the US Open on six occasions. The first was in 1903 when Willie Anderson won the first of his three consecutive titles. Appropriately, the Scottish-born Anderson was Baltusrol's first professional.

Baltusrol has not staged the open since 1980, when Jack Nicklaus shattered US Open records for the lowest 18, 36, 54 and 72 holes in winning his fourth,

and last, title. The PGA Championship has never been played at Baltusrol.

The original course was ploughed up in 1920 to make way for two new courses, the Upper and Lower, which were designed under the supervision of architect A W Tillinghast and opened in 1921. Both have staged the Open although the Upper has done so on just one occasion, in 1936.

The 17th hole on the Lower course is a 630-yard par-5 and is the longest hole ever to be seen in the Open. It is one of the great championship holes.

No course has staged the US Open more times than Baltusrol's six occasions which, uniquely, have been over three different courses.

Right Baltusrol is one of the oldest golf clubs in the United States and, like many others, offers beauty as well as challenging golf.

Below right The tree-lined Lower Course at Baltusrol.

Baltusrol Lower Course

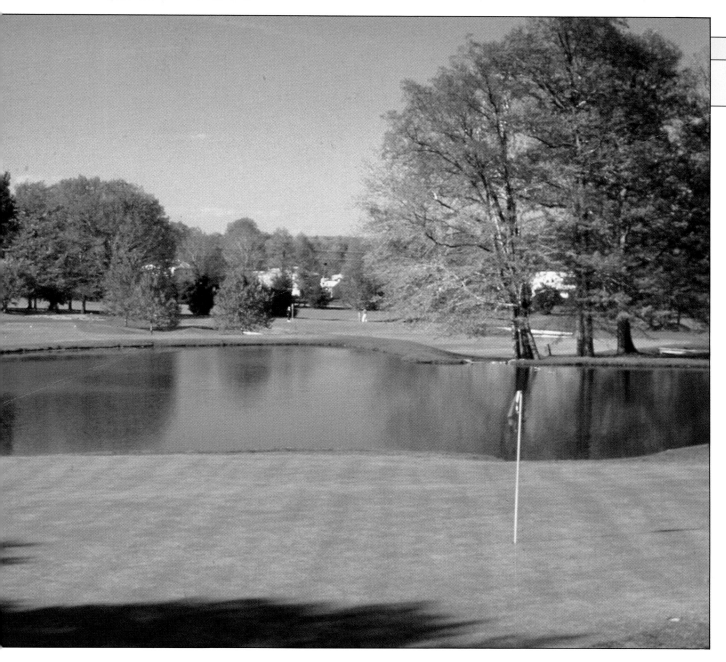

SCORECARD					
Hole	Yards	Par	Hole	Yards	Par
1	478	5	10	454	4
2	381	4	11	428	4
3	443	4	12	193	3
4	194	3	13	393	4
5	393	4	14	409	4
6	470	4	15	430	4
7	505	5	16	216	3
8	374	4	17	630	5
9	205	3	18	542	5
Out	3,443	36	In	3,695	36
TOTALS				7,138	72

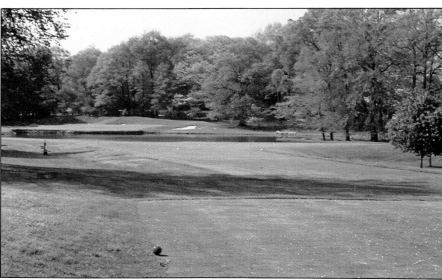

CYPRESS POINT

SITUATED ON THE Monterey peninsula in California and at 6,536 yards, Cypress Point is not a long course but, nevertheless, it is a demanding one. Because of its length it has never been used to stage a major championship.

The course offers great variety to the golfer and its beauty attracts an army of photographers each year. Its 16th hole, like Pebble Beach's 7th, is a definite must for the camera buff.

The hole requires a carry of anything up to 200 yards across the Pacific, on to a green situated on a peninsula high above the ocean, which makes it not only a beautiful hole but a potential disaster. Because of the severity of the 16th many have described Cypress Point as "the best 17-hole golf course in the world"!

It is the 1921 US Women's Amateur Champion Marion Hollins who must take the credit for Cypress Point. She fell in love with California on visiting the area and decided to create a golf course. She raised the cash from local business people and sought the help of course designer Seth Raynor. But Raynor died suddenly, before work on the course was started. Hollins turned to the top designer Alister Mackenzie and in 1928 Cypress Point was opened to the public.

Mackenzie fully utilized the natural surroundings set in the shadow of the Santa Lucia mountains and could have made the course even more spectacular than it is, but he resisted the temptation to create a golf course that was simply beautiful. He wanted to create a demanding test, and did so with great success. To compensate for the course's lack of length he created deceptive greens with many hard-to-read contours.

Left A view of the 15th at Cypress Point with the backdrop of the Pacific Ocean lashing against the rocks.

Right There's no room for error at Cypress Point's 16th.

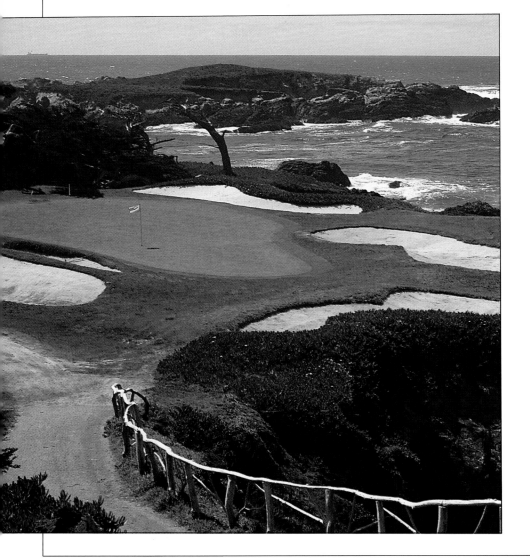

SCORECARD					
Hole	Yards	Par	Hole	Yards	Par
1	421	4	10	480	5
2	548	5	11	437	4
3	162	3	12	404	4
4	384	4	13	365	4
5	493	5	14	388	4
6	518	5	15	143	3
7	168	3	16	231	3
8	363	4	17	393	4
9	292	4	18	346	4
Out	3,349	37	In	3,187	35
TOTALS				6,536	72

INVERNESS

ANOTHER OF AMERICA'S "older generation" golf courses, the Inverness club at Toledo, Ohio, was opened in 1903. Its name came from the Scottish Highland club of the same name but, before naming it, members wrote to its Scottish counterpart seeking permission which was readily granted. And since then a long relationship between the two clubs has existed.

The original club was made up of two nine-hole courses, but in 1919 the Scottish designer Donald Ross merged the two into one 18-holer. A year later the course was considered good enough to stage the US Open and it was won by Ted Ray, the last English winner before Tony Jacklin 50 years later. Ray cut the corner of the dogleg 7th on each of his four rounds and picked up valuable birdies. It was a memorable Open because it was the championship debut for Bobby Jones, Tommy Armour, Gene Sarazen, Leo Diegel and Bill Mehlhorn.

Billy Burke won the Open when next played at Inverness in 1931. It was the longest championship ever, requiring a 72-hole play-off. Dick Mayer won over the revised course

A packed gallery in front of the clubhouse watch the action at Inverness' 18th.

in 1957, and in 1979 Hale Irwin captured his second title despite a final round 75.

Trees, normally a major feature of American courses, are in short supply at Inverness, but to make up for the lack of timber the greens are very exacting and demand to be well read.

DID YOU KNOW?

At that Open in 1920 the Inverness club set a precedent by opening its clubhouse doors to professional golfers, allowing them to use the locker room and other facilities. This was something the great Walter Hagen had been seeking for the professional for some years and he showed his appreciation by making a collection amongst the professional golfers. They presented the club with a clock which was engraved thus:

> God measures men by what they are
> Not what in wealth they possess
> The vibrant message chimes afar
> The voice of Inverness

SCORECARD					
Hole	Yards	Par	Hole	Yards	Par
1	398	4	10	363	4
2	385	4	11	378	4
3	190	3	12	167	3
4	466	4	13	523	5
5	401	4	14	448	4
6	211	3	15	458	4
7	452	4	16	409	4
8	528	5	17	431	4
9	420	4	18	354	4
Out	3,451	35	In	3,531	36
TOTALS				6,982	71

MEDINAH

WHEN ASKED TO name the most difficult championship course in America, most leading professionals will say "Medinah". A look at the scores of the three Open champions at Medinah, 286, 287 and 280, will confirm that its 7,366-yard par-72 is far from easy. It is the longest course ever to be used for the US Open.

The championship course is the Old No. 3, and its tree-lined fairways and many doglegs add to its severity.

The hardest hole on the course is the 171-yard par-3 17th, which requires a drive over part of Lake Kadijah and also a bunker at the front of the green. It was at this hole that Sam Snead took three putts from the edge of the green during the 1949 US Open. He lost the title he was never to win by one stroke to Cary Middlecoff. Lou Graham won the 1975 Open at Medinah after a play-off with John Mahaffey in a tournament interrupted by a violent electrical storm. And in 1990 Hale Irwin

beat Mike Donald, also in a play-off. But what drama there was on the 72nd hole, when Irwin's 45-foot putt to force the play-off took seven seconds to make its journey from clubhead to hole.

The Medinah club was founded in a Chicago suburb in the 1920s as a private club for the Shriners, or the Ancient Arabic Order of Nobles of the Mystic Shrine (see why they're called Shriners?) to give them their full title.

SCORECARD

Hole	Yards	Par	Hole	Yards	Par
1	388	4	10	582	5
2	184	3	11	407	4
3	415	4	12	471	4
4	447	4	13	219	3
5	530	5	14	583	5
6	449	4	15	389	4
7	589	5	16	452	4
8	206	3	17	171	3
9	439	4	18	445	4
Out	3,647	36	In	3,719	36
TOTALS				7,366	72

Medinah No 3 Course

The Old No. 3 course was designed by Tom Bendelow, who intended laying the course out for women's use exclusively. However, at that time it was found to be too difficult for women's play and it was taken over by the male members!

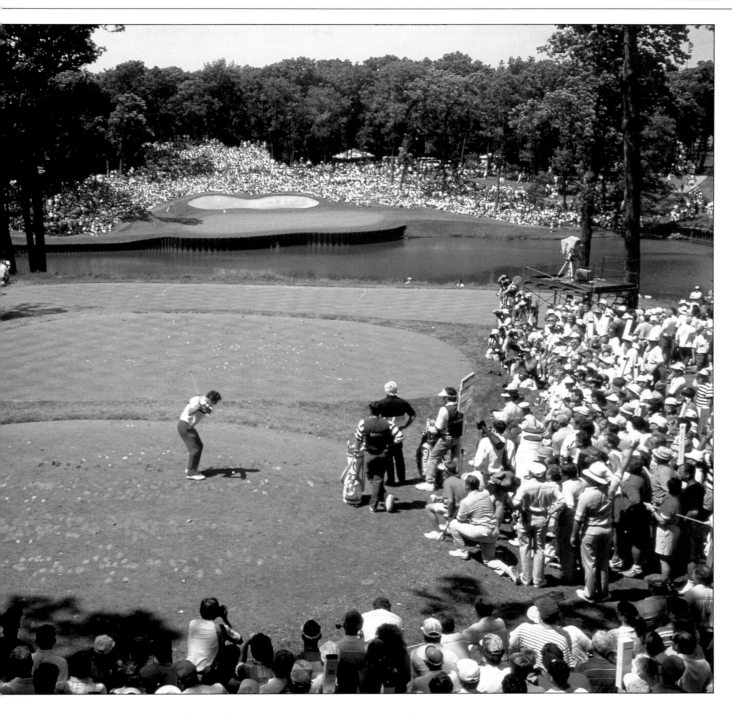

Bendelow's original design left a lot to be desired and many changes have been made over the years to bring this course up to championship standard. After Harry Cooper shot a 63 in winning the 1930 Medinah Open, and before Medinah staged its second US Open in 1975, George Fazio, who was beaten by Ben Hogan after a three-way play-off in the 50th Open at Merion in 1950, was called in to make further changes.

Hale Irwin teeing off while his partner Greg Norman waits at the 17th on the final round of the 1990 US Open at Medinah. Irwin beat Mike Donald in a play-off to capture the title.

MERION

THE MERION COURSE holds the distinction of staging more US Golf Association tournaments than any other course apart from Augusta, which is the permanent home of the Masters.

Merion's long association with championship golf goes back to 1904, when it hosted the US Women's Amateur championship.

Situated at Ardmore, Pennsylvania, the club started life as the Merion Cricket Club in 1865. The first golf course was laid out on a leased piece of land at nearby Haverford in 1896. Originally a nine-hole course, it was expanded to 18 in 1900. Despite this however, it was soon realized that it was too short and not demanding enough for championship golf. The club acquired a new piece of land at Ardmore, its present site, and in 1912 the new course was opened. This became known as the East

Course. A second course was added in 1914.

The East Course, although less than 6,500 yards, is the one used for Championships. This must be a testament to its designer, Hugh Wilson, who created compact and small greens, well-guarded by bunkers. It was the first to be designed by Wilson, but he had spent many years studying championship courses and felt qualified to design his own. He was right.

There are only two par-fives at Merion but coming in the first four holes, at the 2nd and 4th (600 yards), they offer a daunting

SCORECARD

Hole	Yards	Par	Hole	Yards	Par
1	362	4	10	310	4
2	536	5	11	369	4
3	181	3	12	371	4
4	600	5	13	127	3
5	418	4	14	408	4
6	420	4	15	366	4
7	350	4	16	428	4
8	360	4	17	220	3
9	179	3	18	463	4
Out	3,406	36	In	3,062	34
TOTALS				6,468	70

Merion East Course

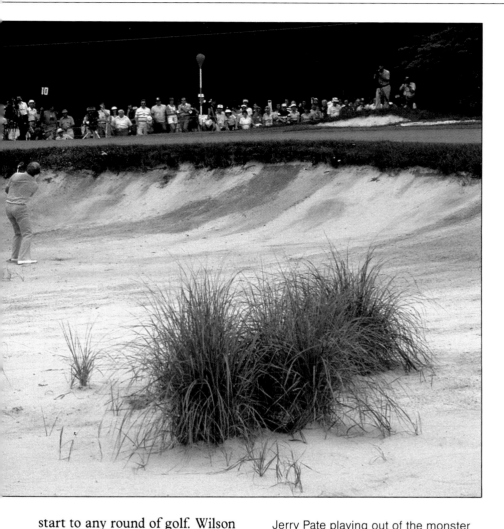

It was Hogan's first Open since an horrific car accident in 1949 that nearly claimed his life. He was told by surgeons he would never walk again, let alone play golf. But, despite being in great discomfort, he achieved the impossible and captured the title.

Lee Trevino beat Jack Nicklaus in a play-off to win the 1971 Open at Merion, and ten years later Australia's David Graham became the first non-American winner since 1960.

Merion was honoured to witness one of golf's greatest occasions. Because it was here on 27 September 1930 that Bobby Jones completed his unique Grand Slam of the Open and Amateur titles of both Britain and America in one year. A plaque alongside the 11th hole commemorates his wonderful achievement.

Merion is notable in that the pin sticks do not have flags on them. Instead they have unique wicker baskets which Hugh Wilson felt would make the course that bit harder, because players wouldn't be able to see which way the wind was blowing.

start to any round of golf. Wilson was a clever man and the shortness of the course is more than compensated for by the strategically-placed bunkers and fast greens. The 8th is probably one of his finest holes. A bunker down the right awaits the short hitter whilst the long hitter is faced with one to the left of the fairway.

Olin Dutra made up an eight-stroke deficit over the last two rounds to take the first Open at Merion in 1934. The club was honoured with the 50th Open in 1950, and what an emotional championship it was, with Ben Hogan taking the title after a three-way play-off with George Fazio and Lloyd Mangrum.

Jerry Pate playing out of the monster bunker alongside Merion's 10th green.

One of Merion's beautiful greens.

MUIRFIELD VILLAGE

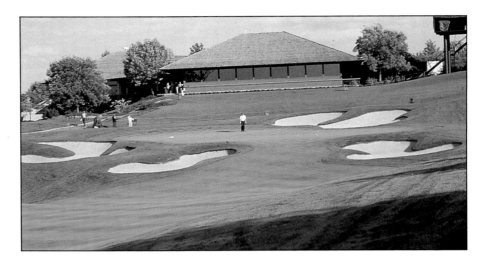

Left The 'Course that Jack Built' – Muirfield Village. So named because it was at the famous Scottish course that Jack Nicklaus had his first British Open win.

THE "COURSE THAT Jack Built", Muirfield Village was the brainchild of Jack Nicklaus and is named after the Scottish course where he won his first British Open in 1966. Jack has designed or helped in the design of many courses, but this is *his* course.

He first considered building his own course in 1966 and, naturally, wanted it to be in his home town of Columbus, Ohio, which is where Muirfield Village is situated. The idea came to him shortly after winning the Masters at Augusta and he pictured it containing some of the beauty of the Augusta National. When he won the British Open three months later the name for his course was chosen.

Despite attempts to talk him into taking his course to a more fashionable part of America, Nicklaus insisted on Columbus. And after raising the necessary finance he called in Peter Dye and Desmond Muirhead to advise with the design. Between them they came up with a course that is stiff enough to test the best of the world's professionals, but offers a fair chance to those people with double-figure handicaps.

They also gave consideration to the spectator in readiness for its use as a championship course, and so many vantage points were created. Nicklaus, Dye and Muirhead left nothing to chance. Yet, in search of perfection, the

SCORECARD					
Hole	Yards	Par	Hole	Yards	Par
1	446	4	10	441	4
2	452	4	11	538	5
3	392	4	12	156	3
4	204	3	13	442	4
5	531	5	14	363	4
6	430	4	15	490	5
7	549	5	16	204	3
8	189	3	17	430	4
9	410	4	18	437	4
Out	3,603	36	In	3,501	36
TOTALS				7,104	72

Above Muirfield Village has shades of Augusta about it. But that is hardly surprising in view of designer Jack Nicklaus' love of the Masters course.

course has undergone many changes over the years.

The Memorial Tournament is the one US Tour event played over Muirfield's 7,104-vard par-72 course. It first took place shortly after the course opened, in 1976, when Roger Maltbie beat Hale Irwin after a play-off. Nicklaus himself won the title in 1977, and again in 1984.

Jack's course hasn't been used for a Major but in 1987 it was the venue for the Ryder Cup, and it was there that history was made when the Americans lost on home soil for the first time when Tony Jacklin's European side clinched a memorable 15-13 win.

Built into the course are many water hazards, which are an integral part of the modern-day golf course. The first five tees are all elevated and most of the shots are downhillers. There are only two uphill shots on the whole course. The greens are superb, but one would expect that from a man like Nicklaus, who is an excellent putter. However, they are far from easy to play.

OAK HILL

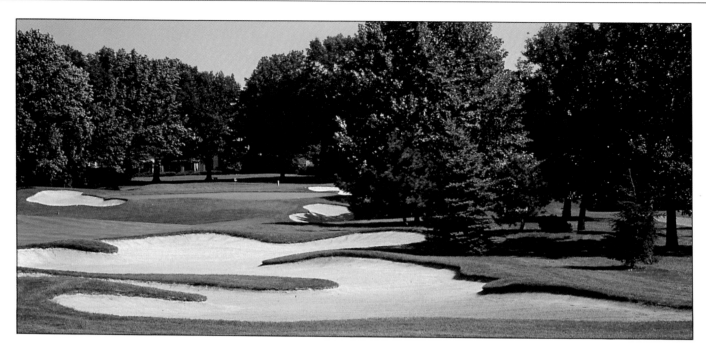

WHAT OAK HILL, at Rochester, New York, offers that many other championship courses do not is three closing holes that will reward the bold and brave yet penalize those not so brave.

On this course, well-placed shots from the tee are essential and these holes have ended many championship dreams in the past. The 16th is particularly evil. Trees line the right side of the fairway while there is a slope to the left. Two bunkers guard the front of the 17th and a fairway bunker catches many out at the 18th. But the approach to the green, which is set on a plateau, requires deadly accuracy or the ball rolls away into a chasm below.

The large white bunkers were the idea of Robert Trent Jones, who re-designed a course originally laid out by Donald Ross.

Oak Hill hosted its first US Open in 1956 when Cary Middlecoff took the title. Hogan lost his chance to 17th when he attempted to clear those two greenside bunkers, which he did, only to see his ball roll off the green.

Lee Trevino equalled the Open record with a 275 when he won Oak Hill's second Open in 1968. And in 1989 Curtis Strange became the first man for 38 years to win back-to-back Opens. Jack Nicklaus, in 1980, won the only US PGA Championship to be played at Oak Hill.

The 18th at Oak Hill with its very difficult approach.

SCORECARD					
Hole	Yards	Par	Hole	Yards	Par
1	377	4	10	408	4
2	436	4	11	479	5
3	420	4	12	303	4
4	145	3	13	448	4
5	381	4	14	210	3
6	543	5	15	413	4
7	442	4	16	474	5
8	156	3	17	208	3
9	365	4	18	441	4
Out	3,265	35	In	3,384	36
TOTALS				6,649	71

OAKLAND HILLS

OAKLAND HILLS, SITUATED at Birmingham, near Detroit, Michigan, is not one of America's most attractive courses, but it certainly offers a varied and stiff test to the golfer.

Shortly before the 1951 US Open at Oakland Hills, the US Golf Association called for the club to make the course a sterner test of the professionals' ability.

Robert Trent Jones was called in, and the course was revamped and modernized. Jones made the fairways narrower, made the rough more severe, and increased the number of bunkers to more than 100. Nothing but the best golf was needed to get anything like par.

Donald Ross designed the original course which was opened in 1918 and the club's first professional, albeit for 12 months, was none other than Walter Hagen. The natural surroundings were ideal for a golf course.

The US Open first came to Oakland Hills in 1924 when English-born Cyril Walker carried off the title. Ralph Guldahl won in 1937 with a record score of 281. Hogan was the champion at

Oakland Hills in 1951, and Gene Littler in 1961. Andy North was champion when the Open was last played there in 1985.

The course has become slightly easier, but it still remains a tough test. The last five holes are the climax and can catch out the unsuspecting golfer at a time when his concentration may just be slipping.

In addition to staging five US Opens, it has twice staged the US Seniors Championship and in 1972 and 1979 hosted the PGA Championship which, coincidentally, were won by two

One of Oakland Hills' large greens well protected by bunkers.

non-Americans, Gary Player of South Africa and Australia's David Graham.

It was Player who played one of Oakland Hills' most memorable shots on his way to winning the title in 1972. Having sliced his tee shot at the 16th at a time when any one of six men could have taken the title, he took a nine-iron from the rough and sent the ball 150 yards over the lake and to within three feet of the pin. He made a birdie and the title was his for the taking.

SCORECARD					
Hole	Yards	Par	Hole	Yards	Par
1	436	4	10	454	4
2	527	5	11	411	4
3	199	3	12	560	5
4	433	4	13	172	3
5	457	4	14	465	4
6	359	4	15	399	4
7	405	4	16	409	4
8	439	4	17	201	3
9	217	3	18	453	4
Out	3,472	35	In	3,524	35
TOTALS				6,996	70

OAKMONT

THE OAKMONT COUNTRY Club near Pittsburgh, Pennsylvania, has hosted the US Open on six occasions. Only Baltusrol has staged it as many times.

Tommy Armour won Oakmont's first Open in 1927 and the last winner was Larry Nelson in 1983. On the third day that year a record crowd for one day at the Open, 38,046, paid to watch the battle between the eventual runner-up Tom Watson and Spain's Severiano Ballesteros.

Oakmont is a test of nerve as well as skill. Players have Henry C Fownes, a local industrialist, who devised and laid out the original course in 1903, to thank for that. Nearly 200 bunkers add to its severity (there were about 220 on the original course) and the greens are regarded as the fastest in America. One of the many bunkers is the infamous Church Pews bunker which measures 40 yards by 60 yards and has nine smaller bunkers within the main one!

Oakmont is regarded as the most difficult 18 holes of golf in America. But in winning the 1973 US Open, Johnny Miller humiliated the course with a record 63 in the final round which, in rain-soaked conditions, was a

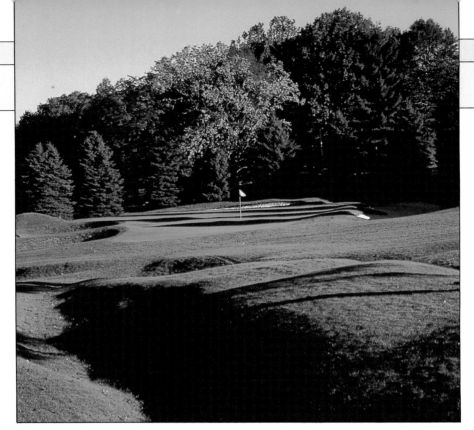

The beautiful 5th at Oakmont.

magnificent achievement. It is widely held to be one of the finest rounds of golf ever witnessed in America.

Oakmont's first major championship was the 1919 US Amateur Championship. The beaten finalist that day was Bobby Jones. When it was next held there Jones became champion.

Work on Oakmont started in the autumn of 1903 and within six weeks the first 12 holes were

completed. Fownes' dream of creating "the hardest golf course it was possible to design" was well under way. The following autumn all 18 holes were ready for play.

In 1987 Oakmont became a National Historic Landmark, the only golf course in the United States to be so designated.

SCORECARD					
Hole	Yards	Par	Hole	Yards	Par
1	469	4	10	462	4
2	343	4	11	371	4
3	425	4	12	603	5
4	561	5	13	185	3
5	379	4	14	360	4
6	201	3	15	453	4
7	434	4	16	228	3
8	240	3	17	322	4
9	480	5	18	456	4
Out	3,532	36	In	3,440	35
TOTALS				6,972	71

OLYMPIC CLUB

EVERYWHERE YOU LOOK at the Olympic Club on the western edge of San Francisco you can see nothing but trees. In fact the course is adorned with approximately 30,000 of them.

At the turn of the century the site was mostly sand dunes and had virtually no trees. Now, some of them are over 100 feet tall. The site is between Lake Merced and the Pacific Ocean. However, despite its proximity, the ocean cannot be seen from the Lakeside Course - hardly surprising, with all those trees!

However, the other course, the Ocean Course, commands some breathtaking views across the ocean. But it is not suitable for championship golf.

A shortage of bunkers, fairway and greenside gives the impression the course is easy. It is not. The par-4s offer a great deal of variety and reaching them in regulation two offers the toughest of tests even for the professionals. In the 3rd hole, the Lakeside Course has one of the great golf holes. It is not hard - it is a 223-yard downhill par-3. But standing on the elevated tee you have breathtaking views of San Francisco and the Golden Gate Bridge.

The moist San Francisco atmosphere reduces carry and roll which is something many newcomers overlook.

It was at the Olympic in 1966 that Arnold Palmer threw away a seemingly invincible lead of seven shots in the Open, before making a remarkable comeback at the 18th from deep rough to force a play-off with Billy Casper - only to lose by four shots the next day!

What a magnificent sight! A packed crowd around the 8th watching Bernhard Langer in action during the 1987 US Open at the Olympic Club. Scott Simpson was the surprise winner.

The 18th at Olympic is one of golf's great spectator holes. The small green sits in the corner of a horseshoe-shaped fairway set in a dip, giving wonderful banked vantage points.

SCORECARD					
Hole	Yards	Par	Hole	Yards	Par
1	533	5	10	422	4
2	394	4	11	430	4
3	223	3	12	390	4
4	438	4	13	186	3
5	457	4	14	417	4
6	437	4	15	149	3
7	288	4	16	609	5
8	137	3	17	522	5
9	433	4	18	343	4
Out	3,340	35	In	3,468	36
TOTALS				6,808	71

Olympic Lakeside Course

PEBBLE BEACH

FOR A COMBINATION of beauty, the spectacular and an exciting golf course Pebble Beach stands head and shoulders above the rest.

Situated on the Monterey peninsula approximately 120 miles south of San Francisco, it was the first of many superb golf courses to be built in the area. The others, Cypress Point, Monterey and Spyglass Hill, all followed later.

Pebble Beach was opened in 1919 and was the idea of Samuel Morse, the nephew of the man who invented Morse code. Morse bought the land from the Southern Pacific Railroad Company and to help him develop the course he obtained the services of Jack

Neville who, surprisingly, was *not* a golf course designer but a real estate salesman. Nevertheless, they produced an excellent golf course spreading from the cliffs along the coastline inland to the edge of the Del Monte Forest.

The 7th hole ranks as one of the most beautiful, and certainly most photographed, holes in the world.

It is a par-3 measuring little over 100 yards. But what a setting! The green is set on its own, jutting out into the Pacific Ocean. But there are other great holes at Pebble Beach. The second shot to the 8th requires a carry over a 100-foot drop into the Ocean

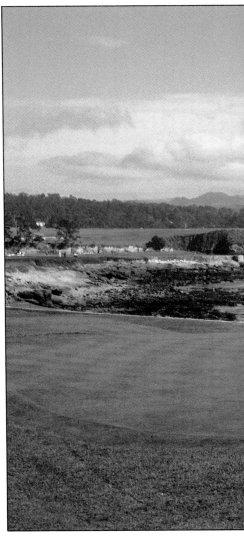

Above Pebble Beach's 18th hole is probably one of the toughest closing holes in Championship golf.

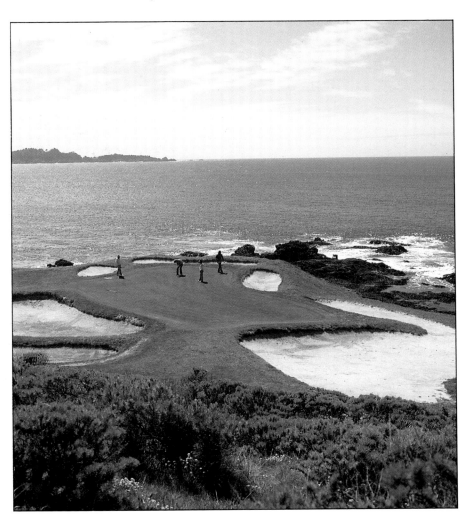

Left One of golf's most photographed holes, the 7th at Pebble Beach.

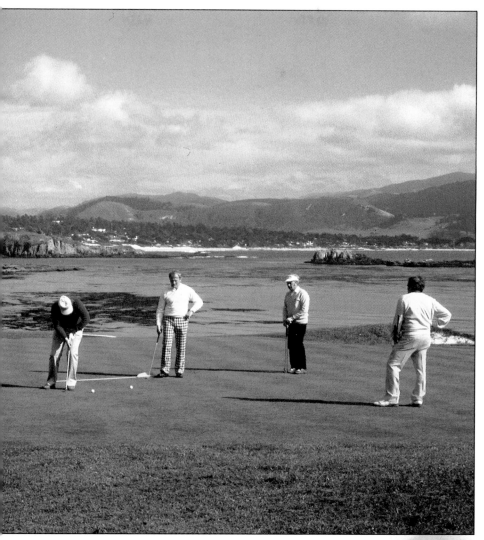

below. And the 18th along the rocky coastline is probably one of the best finishing holes in golf. To any championship-winning aspirant, the task of making par at each of the last two holes is one of the most daunting prospects in the game.

But Tom Watson tore those last two holes apart when winning his first US Open in 1982. He required two pars to force a play-off with Jack Nicklaus, but birdies gave him the title by two strokes.

That was only the second time Pebble Beach had played host to the US Open; its location, 120 miles from the nearest big city, has limited its use as a Major venue.

It first hosted the Open in 1972 when Jack Nicklaus won his third title, and it played host for a third time in 1992. Lanny Wadkins captured his first Major, the PGA Championship, at Pebble Beach in 1977.

Despite only holding four Majors, the Californian course is one of the three used for the AT&T National Pro-am, which is one of the US Tour events each year. It was previously known as the Bing Crosby Pro-am.

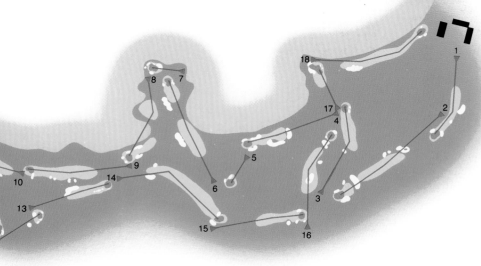

SCORECARD

Hole	Yards	Par	Hole	Yards	Par
1	373	4	10	426	4
2	502	5	11	384	4
3	388	4	12	202	3
4	327	4	13	392	4
5	166	3	14	565	5
6	516	5	15	397	4
7	107	3	16	402	4
8	431	4	17	209	3
9	464	4	18	548	5
Out	3,274	36	In	3,525	36
TOTALS				6,799	72

PINEHURST

THERE ARE SEVEN courses at Pinehurst in North Carolina, but by far the best is the No. 2 course.

The inaugural nine hole course was laid out in 1898 by James Tufts, a Boston pharmacist. He had previously acquired a 5,000 acre site, so land was no problem. A year later it was extended to 18 holes. And after Harry Vardon played the course during his visit to America in 1900, golf took off in the area. It was then that Tufts called for the services of Scotsman Donald Ross.

Ross arrived to take up duties as golfing coach in 1900, but most of his time was spent designing four more courses for the area.

The No. 2 was completed in 1907 and in 1910 the No. 3 course arrived on the scene. And when No. 4 was opened in 1919 Pinehurst became the first American club to have four courses. But it went one better in 1950 when the fifth course was opened shortly after Ross's death. Since then two more courses have been added and Pinehurst can rightly claim to be the biggest golfing centre in America.

Pinehurst staged the PGA Championship in 1936, its only Major, when Denny Shute beat Jimmy Thomson in the final. Since then, the biggest event to be played over the North Carolina course was the 1951 Ryder Cup.

The World Golf Hall of Fame is situated at Pinehurst and was inaugurated in 1974 by President Gerald Ford, himself a keen golfer. Between 1903 and 1950 Pinehurst hosted the North and South Open and it was here in 1940 that Ben Hogan won his first ever US Tour event.

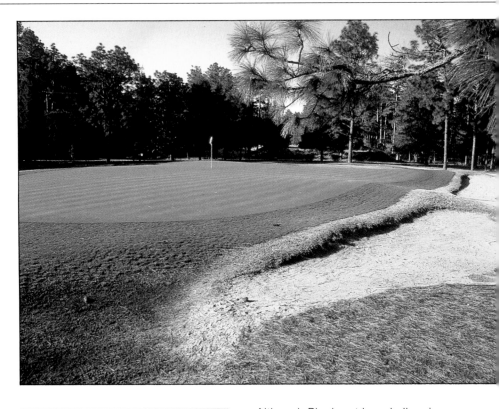

SCORECARD

Hole	Yards	Par	Hole	Yards	Par
1	373	4	10	454	5
2	167	3	11	335	4
3	340	4	12	137	3
4	526	5	13	360	4
5	372	4	14	372	4
6	361	4	15	478	5
7	353	4	16	314	4
8	486	5	17	178	3
9	120	3	18	402	4
Out	3,098	36	In	3,030	36
TOTALS				6,128	72

Pinehurst No 2 Course

Although Pinehurst is a challenging course, it is not used as a Championship course because of its rural location.

PINE VALLEY

PINE VALLEY IS one of the truly spectacular golf courses, with its 2nd hole being one of the game's great holes.

It is only a 367-yard par-4 but, as you stand on the tee looking at the green, the fairway is littered with bunkers. The view is spectacular and the temptation is to photograph the fairway rather than attempt to play it.

But the 2nd is just one of 18 holes at Pine Valley with its own individual characteristics, adding to the overall beauty of the course.

Located in New Jersey at Clementon, the course was originally developed by George Crump, owner of the Colonnades Hotel, Philadelphia, who wanted to fulfil a dream of building the best and toughest golf course in the world. He was assisted in the design by British architect H S Colt, and they developed the course around a previously untouched 184 acres of forest area in southern New Jersey. The sandy soil made design a lot easier.

Crump is said to have spotted the land while making a train journey from Philadelphia to Atlantic City and immediately decided it was the location for his "dream". The land was once the home of an encampment occupied by the Delaware Indians.

In 1912 Crump persuaded 18 friends each to invest $1,000 and they purchased the land.

The course opened in 1916 as a 14-hole course and was immediately hailed as one of the most demanding in America, if not the world. And that is a belief many golfers still hold today, as accuracy to avoid the bunkers and trees is crucial at every hole. It became a full 18-hole course in 1919, but Crump never lived to see the completion of his dream. He had died the previous year.

What makes Pine Valley tougher than most courses is the lack of fairways as such. Each tee shot has to land on a pre-determined area which, in most cases, is large enough to hit. But poor shots are heavily penalized because of the severe rough.

Fear hits you the first time you play Pine Valley. Just looking around at the trees and bunkers is enough to make you want to put your clubs away and spend the day playing the 19th hole 18 times instead!

Club members are willing to take bets that nobody, amateur or professional, will break 80 the first time they play Pine Valley.

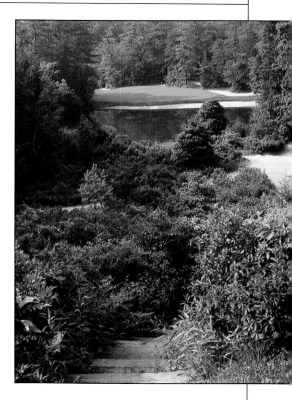

Despite its beautiful setting, Pine Valley is still waiting to host its first Major.

SCORECARD

Hole	Yards	Par	Hole	Yards	Par
1	427	4	10	146	3
2	367	4	11	392	4
3	181	3	12	344	4
4	444	4	13	448	4
5	232	3	14	184	3
6	388	4	15	591	5
7	567	5	16	433	4
8	319	4	17	338	4
9	427	4	18	428	4
Out	3,352	35	In	3,304	35
TOTALS				6,656	70

SHINNECOCK HILLS

FORMED IN 1891, Shinnecock Hills has been in existence ever since and, consequently, is one of the longest-surviving clubs in the United States.

Scotsman Willie Dunn laid out the original course and on completion he became the club's first professional. Dunn's original course was styled on Scottish design and his ancestry is very evident.

Situated at Southampton, Long Island, Shinnecock Hills can boast the oldest clubhouse in the United States, dating back to 1892. It was also the first 18-hole course in America. The course is named after the Shinnecock tribe of Indians who once lived in the area.

It hosted the second ever US Open in 1896 but it had to wait ninety years to stage its next championship. And it was on that occasion that Raymond Floyd

Above A view of the 9th and 18th greens at Shinnecock Hills, the first 18-hole golf course in the United States.

Right A superb view across the Shinnecock Hills links with the 18th, the 'Home' hole in the foreground.

\multicolumn{6}{c}{**SCORECARD**}
Hole	Yards	Par	Hole	Yards	Par
1	391	4	10	412	4
2	221	3	11	158	3
3	456	4	12	469	4
4	382	4	13	366	4
5	512	5	14	447	4
6	456	4	15	400	4
7	184	3	16	519	5
8	361	4	17	169	3
9	411	4	18	426	4
Out	3,374	35	In	3,366	35
TOTALS				6,740	70

became the oldest champion at 43 years 284 days.

The idea of a golf course in New York came when William Vanderbilt, of the famous family of the same name, saw Dunn play an exhibition match in Biarritz. Upon his return to New York the millionaire discussed his plans with friends and when they decided to go ahead he contacted Dunn, who made the trip across the Atlantic.

Dunn set about looking for a suitable site, which he found set amongst sandhills close to the sea. It was reminiscent of the east coast of Scotland where he used to live.

The course was ready for use in the summer of 1891 and when Stanford White was called in to design a luxurious clubhouse,

Shinnecock Hills rightly claimed to be the best golf club in America.

As the game gained in popularity so did the exclusivity of the Shinnecock Hills club and members had to wear red coats when playing - a rule that had existed in Britain in the early days of golf.

While some of the present-day course bears some of Dunn's traits a lot of it now dates to the early 1930s, when Dick Wilson made many changes because its length of only just 5,000 yards was far too short for the game in the 1930s, and it certainly would not gain championship status again unless changes were made. The final hole, perhaps the toughest on the course, certainly bears a

resemblance to Dunn's early design; it is very British with an undulating fairway, severe rough on both sides, and with a strong wind often blowing across it.

SHINNECOCK HILLS' 18 HOLES	
1 Westward Ho!	10 Eastward Ho!
2 Plateau	11 Hill Head
3 Peconic	12 Tuckahoe
4 Pump House	13 Road Side
5 Montauk	14 Thom's Elbow
6 The Pond	15 Sebonac
7 Redan	16 Shinnecock
8 Lowlands	17 Eden
9 Ben Nevis	18 Home

WINGED FOOT

WINGED FOOT IS one of America's best-known courses. Situated at Mamaroneck, north of New York, it was founded in the 1920s by members of the New York Athletic Club and it was from their emblem that the club's name was taken.

The club boasts two 18-hole courses, East and West, and while it is the longer West Course which is used for championship golf, many members prefer the East Course. Architect A W Tillinghast had the responsibility of designing the course and in doing so he gave the New York Athletic Club members something to think about because the West Course was one of the toughest in America. Both opened in 1923.

What makes Winged Foot particularly difficult is the length of the par-4s. Seven of them are over 440 yards, and even the best players sometimes have difficulty in reaching the greens in the regulation number of strokes.

The US Open was first played at Winged Foot in 1929 and Bobby Jones captured his third title. His score of 14 *over* par certainly highlights how severe the West Course was. And when Billy Casper became the second Open champion at Winged Foot 30 years later he needed to single putt no fewer than 31 greens in order to keep his score *down* to 282. It was during Casper's triumph that violent thunderstorms caused a day's abandonment for the first time in Open history.

Hale Irwin beat a very difficult course to win after a play-off in 1974 and in 1984 another play-off was required as Fuzzy Zoeller beat Greg Norman.

Jack Nicklaus maintained for many years that Winged Foot's 17th was the greatest match of a golfer's skill against that of the designer. It requires a long accurate drive amid trees, followed by a long second shot to a green well protected by bunkers. The hole is known as Well Well - I'm sure it has been called other things at times.

Right Fuzzy Zoeller, Greg Norman, and a very large crowd around the 13th green during the 1984 US Open at Winged Foot. Zoeller beat Norman by eight strokes in a play-off to take his first title.

Below Zoeller playing out of a bunker on his way to winning his title in 1984.

\ SCORECARD					
Hole	Yards	Par	Hole	Yards	Par
1	446	4	10	190	3
2	411	4	11	386	4
3	216	3	12	535	5
4	453	4	13	212	3
5	515	5	14	418	4
6	324	4	15	417	4
7	166	3	16	457	4
8	442	4	17	449	4
9	471	4	18	448	4
Out	3,444	35	In	3,512	35
TOTALS				6,956	70

Winged Foot West Course

GOLFING TERMINOLOGY

ACE See *Hole-in-One*.

ADDRESS Once a player has taken up his *stance* and *grounded* the clubhead behind the ball he is said to have *addressed* the ball. Note that the clubhead must *not* be grounded in a *bunker*.

ALBATROSS A score of three strokes *under par* for a *hole*. An albatross is very rare, even amongst the leading professionals. Also known as a *Double Eagle*.

APPROACH A shot made from the *fairway* onto, or towards, the *green*.

APRON The area surrounding the *green* that is cut shorter than the *fairway* but not quite as short as the *putting surface*. Also known as the *fringe*.

BACK NINE The last nine holes of an 18-hole round. Also known as the *Inward Half*.

BACKSWING A very important part of the golf swing. It is when the clubhead is taken away from its *address* position to the top of the arc, before the *downswing* and eventual contact with the ball. If the backswing is all wrong, then there is little chance of getting the rest of the *swing* right.

BEST BALL A form of competition when one player competes against two or three others and the score of the individual player is matched against the best score of the other players. It can be adapted to both *match-* and *strokeplay* golf.

BETTER BALL A match involving four players, two on each side, and the better ball of each pair counts at each hole. Again it can be used in *match-* or *strokeplay* conditions.

BIRDIE A score of one stroke *under par* for a *hole*.

BOGEY (a) One stroke *over par* for a *hole*. A double bogey is two over par and triple bogey three over par. (b) The number of strokes a good player is expected to need to complete one hole, or the complete round. The term bogey is often replaced by the more popular term *par* these days.

BUNKER A sand-filled hollow strategically placed on the course - normally where you want to hit your ball! Also known as *traps*. The rules state that you must not *ground* your clubhead during *address* when in a bunker and, as a matter of courtesy to other golfers, all marks made by the golfer in a bunker must be raked over on leaving it.

CARRY The distance covered by the golf ball from the point where it was hit to the point where it first lands.

CASUAL WATER A temporary accumulation of water on the golf course. A player may move his ball from casual water without penalty.

CHIP A low trajectory/lofted shot normally over some form of obstacle - bunker, tree, water etc - and usually made onto or towards the *green*.

CLOSED STANCE A position whereby the left foot is slightly forward of the right one at *address*.

CUT A type of spin imparted on the ball which causes it to travel to the right. It is often the cause of the slice. Also the term used when the field in a tournament is reduced from its original number. In most professional tournaments the field is cut after 54 and 72 holes.

DIVOT A piece of turf cut out of

the ground while playing a shot. Divots are usually cut with lofted clubs like 9-irons and wedges when it is necessary to impart backspin on the ball. Divots must be replaced, and if you are walking the course and find an unplaced divot don't walk past it - replace it. If everybody did that once on every round then golf courses would be in a much better condition.

DOGLEG A *fairway* that has a change of direction from *tee* to *green* is described as a dogleg.

DID YOU KNOW?

It is believed that the birdie became so named when Abe Smith, playing at Atlantic City in the United States at the turn of the 20th century, played his second shot to a par-4 within inches of the hole. He then turned to his playing partners and said: "That was one bird of a shot."

The term eagle was also first used in the United States but not until the 1920s and, because the eagle is a splendid bird, it was appropriately used to describe a hole played in one stroke better than a plain birdie. For the same reason albatross was probably chosen to describe a hole played in one stroke better than an eagle.

DORMIE In *matchplay* golf a player or team is said to be dormie when they cannot lose. If, for example, they are leading by two holes and there are two holes to play then they are said to be "dormie two".

DOUBLE EAGLE See *Albatross*.

DOWNSWING Following the *takeaway* of the club from the *address* position to the top of the *backswing*, the next action is the downswing which, like all other aspects of the *swing*, is very important.

DRAW A controlled shot that makes the ball travel initially to the right of the target but then deliberately turn left towards it.

DRIVE A shot made from the *tee*, usually with a driver or wooden club, although many of today's professionals tend to drive with long irons.

DROPPING THE BALL During a round a player may have to drop the ball, either because it is unplayable or it has landed on ground under repair and must be moved so as not to cause damage. The rules governing the dropping of a ball are very strict. At one time the drop was made from over the player's shoulder; now it is made from in front of the player with an outstretched arm.

EAGLE Two shots *under par* for a *hole*.

FADE A controlled shot like the *draw* but with the ball initially veering left of its target before turning right towards it.

FAIRWAY The area between *tee* and *green*. Both sides of the fairway are often bound by natural hazards such as trees, bushes or longer grass known as the *rough*. The fairway is the cut area

between the teeing ground and green, but is not cut as finely as the green.

FLIGHT OF THE BALL As its name implies, it is the path taken by the ball while in flight. There are many different flight paths the ball can take. There is the *straight* flight, *slice* and *hook*, *push* and *pull*, and *draw* and *fade*.

FOLLOW-THROUGH The action of allowing the clubhead to continue its *swing* after making contact with the ball.

FORE! A shout made by golfers to warn fellow golfers on the course that a ball may be heading towards them.

FOUR BALL A match involving four players, usually playing in pairs. The better ball of each pair can decide each *hole* or the aggregate scores can decide the winners.

FOURSOMES A match involving four players divided into two teams who use one ball each and take it in turns to play shots at their respective ball.

FRESH AIR SHOT A shot played at the ball but misses. It counts as one *stroke*. Also known as the *air stroke*.

FRINGE Also known as an *apron*.

FRONT NINE The first nine holes of an 18-hole round. Also known as the *Outward Half*.

GIMMIE A term used when a player allows his opponent a *putt* without playing the ball. It is a sporting gesture and usually made when there is little danger of the putt being missed.

GREEN The finely manicured *putting surface* which one aims to reach in the least number of

DID YOU KNOW?

Before the advent of lawn mowers, golf course greens were kept in shape by grazing sheep and hungry rabbits.

strokes from the *teeing* area. Greens are well cared for and for this reason must be treated with respect. Don't take *trolley carts* on to the green, replace all *pitch* marks made by balls landing on the green and, like *divots*, if you see an unrepaired pitch mark, don't leave it, repair it.

GRIP That part of the club shaft that is held by the golfer. The hold you take on the club is often incorrectly referred to as "the grip".

GROSS SCORE The score achieved by a player in a *strokeplay* or *medalplay* round before his *handicap* is deducted.

GROUNDING THE CLUB Once the clubhead has been placed on the ground behind the ball at *address* it is said to be grounded.

GROUND UNDER REPAIR Golf courses are continuously undergoing repair to make them better places to play on. GUR areas are appropriately marked and balls landing therein must be removed, but without penalty.

HALVE, TO In *matchplay* to play a *hole* in the same number of strokes as the opposing player or team results in the hole being "halved".

HANDICAPPING Handicap systems vary so much from club-to-club and country-to-country that it would be impossible to analyse them in such a short space. However, if you take up the sport seriously, you should enquire at your local club about obtaining an official handicap. Without one you will not be able to compete in many competitions and tournaments.

HAZARDS The rules of golf describe a hazard as a *bunker* or water hazard only. But other things like roads, walls, trees, bushes etc are certainly hazardous if you come across them during a round of golf.

HOLD The position of one's hands on the *grip* of the golf club. The hold is often incorrectly referred to as "the grip".

DID YOU KNOW?

The longest recorded hole-in-one was achieved by Robert Mitera at the appropriately named Miracle Hill golf course at Omaha, Nebraska in 1965. A two-handicap player, Mitera's drive at the 409m (447yd) downhill 10th hole landed in the hole. He was aided by a tailwind!

HOLE That 4¼in (12cm) diameter target that is placed on the *green* and which all golfers are striving to reach in the least number of shots. As the hole's position on the green is changed frequently, its situation is shown by a flag on a pole, so players can see where to play their *approach* shots.

HOLE-IN-ONE Playing a hole-in-one shot direct from the *teeing* area. It is normally done only at *par-3 holes* although a hole-in-one has been recorded at a 447-yard par-4 hole. Also known as an *Ace.*

HOLING OUT The final act of putting the ball into the *hole.*

HONOUR The rules dictate that the person or team winning the previous *hole* has the "honour" of going first at the next hole. If the hole is halved then the person having the honour at the previous hole retains it.

HOOK A hooked shot is generally the result of an error. The ball heads towards the target before changing direction and heading well left of the target.

IN PLAY A ball is in play from the moment it is struck from the *teeing* area.

INWARD HALF The last nine holes of an 18-hole round of golf. Also known as the *Back Nine.*

LATERAL WATER HAZARD Lateral water hazards are marked with red marker posts and are water hazards that run parallel to the fairway, thus making it impossible to drop the ball behind the hazard as per the normal rules. In the case of lateral water hazards the ball must be dropped within two club lengths of where it entered the hazard, but not nearer to the *hole.*

LIE The position where the ball comes to rest is known as the lie.

LINKS Strictly speaking, any area where golf is played can be termed as the "links". But it is generally a term only used to define a golf course adjacent to the coast.

LOCAL RULES All golf clubs, in addition to the recognized Rules of Golf, have Local Rules which must be adhered to. Local Rules are printed on the scorecards and must be read before a round.

LOST BALL A ball is deemed to be lost if not found within five minutes of starting to look for it.

MATCHPLAY A form of competition whereby one team or individual attempts to win more *holes* than the other. The person or team winning a hole goes one up, two up and so on until there are not enough holes left for the opponent to be able to win. Halved holes do not affect the score.

MEDALPLAY Another name for *strokeplay.*

NET SCORE A player's score after the deduction of his *handicap* from his gross score.

OFF SCRATCH A player is said to be "off scratch" when he or she plays to no handicap.

OPEN STANCE An open stance is when the left foot is drawn back slightly from the line of flight.

OUT OF BOUNDS Certain areas of a golf course are designated as Out of Bounds and are indicated by white marker posts. Any ball that goes out of bounds must be replayed at the position from which it was originally played, with the addition of a one-stroke penalty.

OUTWARD HALF The first nine holes of an 18-hole round of golf. Also known as the *Front Nine*.

OVER PAR A score of more than the *par* figure for a *hole* or round.

PAR The par figure for each hole. It is the score an expert golfer would be expected to complete it in. Length decides par figures and assumes that top players would two *putt* on each green so, for example, it would be assumed a leading professional would reach a 197-yard green in one shot and then two putt. It would therefore be designated a par-3.

PIN HIGH A ball is pin high when it is level with the flag but either to the right or left of it.

PITCH A shot played with a lofted club high into the air so that the ball lands on the *green*. Depending on conditions, the ball will either stop dead on hitting the *putting surface*, or will land and then run-on after pitching. The softer the putting surface, the more chance there is of the ball stopping dead.

PITCH MARK When a ball is hit with a lofted club towards the *green* it will leave a pitch mark in the green upon landing. Always repair any pitch marks your ball makes.

PLUGGED BALL A ball that remains in its own *pitch mark* is said to be plugged. This happens most often in *bunkers* but can also happen on *fairways* if they are very soft after a downpour of rain.

PREFERRED LIES During the winter months, but occasionally at other times, the local rules will state that preferred lies are allowed on the *fairways*. This rule is to protect the fairway from undue wear in bad weather and

your ball can be moved to a good piece of ground, normally only a few inches away from its original landing place, but not nearer to the *hole*.

PULL A shot that goes to the left but, unlike the *hook*, does not start by going to the right first.

PUSH A shot that goes to the right but, unlike the *slice*, does not start by going to the left first.

PUTT The action of attempting to get the ball into the hole from on the *putting surface* by using the putter.

PUTTING GREEN (PUTTING SURFACE) The correct name for the *green*.

RECEIVE A BYE To be exempt from the first round of a competition thus going straight into the second.

ROUGH The uncut area adjacent to the *fairway*. The first bit of rough is usually the "light rough" or "semi rough" while the remainder is the "deep rough".

SHAFT The part of the golf club between the handle and the clubhead.

SLICE A sliced shot is usually the result of an error. The ball heads towards the target before changing direction and heading well right of its intended target.

STABLEFORD A form of competition based on a points system which allows one point for a *hole* played in one *stroke* over *par*, two points if played in *par*, three points for a *birdie*, four for an *eagle* and five for an *albatross*.

STANCE The position a player adopts when addressing the ball. It is very important to make sure the correct stance is adopted.

STROKE A stroke is when the club is moved forward with the intention of hitting the ball. If it does not hit it (see *Fresh Air Shot*) it still counts as one stroke.

STRAIGHT FLIGHT When the ball travels in a straight line whilst in flight.

STROKE INDEX Each *hole* is graded according to its stroke index and is clearly indicated on the scorecard. The most difficult hole on the course is stroke 1 while the easiest is stroke 18.

STROKEPLAY The simplest form of competition whereby each player's, or team's, aggregate strokes for the round are calculated and the appropriate deductions are then made for *handicap(s)*.

SWING The swing is the most important part of the game of golf. A bad swing will almost certainly result in bad golf. The swing is the action of taking the club away from the *address* position, up through the *backswing*, into the *downswing* and then into contact with the ball. It doesn't sound much, but there is an awful lot to the golf swing as you will find out.

TAKEAWAY The first movement of the clubhead when it is taken away from the ball at the *address* position.

TEE The small plastic or wooden aid on which the ball is placed when playing from the *teeing ground*.

TEEING GROUND Normally raised, it is clearly marked and it is from the teeing ground that each *hole* begins. Ladies have tees forward from the men, and there is normally a third teeing ground at each hole set aside for competitions. Two markers clearly indicate from where tee shots must be played and they must be from between and behind the markers.

DID YOU KNOW?

The special prize for a hole-in-one at the 8th hole during the 1985 New South Wales Open was either £5,000 in cash, or a pre-paid funeral with a monument. The prize was offered by local PGA director, and funeral parlour owner, Paul Smith . . . it is not known whether the event went to a sudden death play-off!

Trolleys or golf bags should not be taken on to the teeing ground.

TENDING THE FLAG When putting from on the putting surface the flag must be *out* of the hole before the ball enters the hole. However, if the ball is a fair distance from the hole the flag may be left in and tended by another player who must ensure it is removed before the ball enters the hole.

THREE BALL A match involving three players who play against each other.

THREESOME A match when one player plays against two others who, in turn, take shots at the same ball.

TOPPED BALL A ball is "topped" when the top half, instead of the bottom half, is struck with the club. The most common cause for topping a ball is a player moving his head during the *swing*.

TOUR A series of tournaments usually spread over a full season, for professional golfers. There are Tours in many different parts of the world, but the US PGA Tour and the PGA European Tour are the two biggest.

TRAP See *bunker.*

TROLLEY CARTS An aid for carrying the golf bag around the course. Most clubs offer a trolley hire service and the more exclusive clubs have electric carts or buggies for hire. But they seem to defeat part of the object of playing golf . . . the taking of exercise.

UNDER PAR A score of less strokes than the *par* figure for a *hole* or round.

WATER HAZARDS The Rules of Golf define a water hazard as any

"sea, lake, pond, river, ditch, surface drainage ditch, or other open water course, whether it contains water or not, and anything of a similar nature". Water hazards are marked by yellow posts or lines. (See *Lateral Water Hazards.*)

WINTER GREEN To protect the greens in the winter months, temporary greens are often cut out of the *fairway*. They are not manicured as well as the normal greens but without them many courses would be forced to close during the winter months as the greens could easily get damaged during the adverse weather.

CONVERSION TABLE

Both imperial and metric measurements have been used throughout the book as these vary from one golf club to another. To help you convert measurements please see the table below.

Yards	Metres
110	100
164	150
219	200
273	250
328	300
383	350
437	400
492	450
547	500
601	550
656	600
711	650
766	700
820	750
875	800
930	850
984	900
1039	950
1094	1000
2187	2000
3281	3000
4374	4000
5468	5000

INDEX

ACKNOWLEDGEMENTS

Quarto would like to thank the following for providing photographs, and for permission to reproduce copyright material. While every effort has been made to trace and acknowledge all copyright holders, we would like to apologise should there have been any omissions.

Key: (t) = top; (b) = below; (l) = left; (r) = right; (m) = middle; (both) = both photographs on the page.

Baltusrol Golf Club, page: 129 (both).

Peter Dazeley Golf Photography, pages: 33, 37, 43, 44(l), 45(t), 48(t), 49(tr), 50(both), 51(both), 53(r), 54(l), 55(b), 57(both), 58, 60(tr & b both), 61(r), 63(t), 65(b), 67, 70(t), 70(bl), 74, 77, 78(br), 79(l), 81(b), 90, 92(b), 96(both), 97, 98, 99, 100, 101(t), 112, 114, 116(t), 117, 119(t), 121(r), 126(b), 130, 131, 144, 145.

Mansell Collection, pages: 8(t), 9, 10.

Mark Newcombe/ Visions in Golf, pages: 7, 8(both), 11, 12, 14(l), 15(t), 15(m & b), 16, 28, 34, 35, 41, 44(r), 45(b), 46(b), 47(l), 48(br), 49(b), 52(b), 54(both), 16, 58-9, 60(tl), 61(t & bl), 62, 63(b), 64, 68(t), 69(both), 72(t), 73, 82(r), 75(all three), 76, 79(r), 92, 93, 94, 95(all three), 101(b), 102, 103, 108, 109, 110, 111, 113, 114(both), 116(tr), 118(l), 119(r), 120, 121(b), 125, 126(t), 127, 132, 138, 139, 140, 141, 142.

P.G.A. World Golf Hall of Fame; pages: 6-7, 72.

St. Andrews University Library, pages: 13, 14(main), 15(t), 44(t), 46(t), 47(r), 64(t), 65(t), 73(both).

Phil Sheldon Golf Picture Library, pages: 40, 42, 49(tl), 52(t), 53(l), 70(br), 71, 78(t), 80, 81(t), 82, 85, 86, 87, 89, 91, 104, 106,-8(both), 115, 122-3, 130, 135, 137(both), 143, 146, 147, 148(both), 157(both).

US Golf Association, pages: 54(b), 68(b).

Volvo Marketing, page: 59.

The author would like to thank John Rollason of Poniente Golf Club, Mallorca, for his invaluable assistance with the instructional part of this book.